Dedicated to my lovely, sassy, in

With special thanks and gratitud
hundreds of hours of benevolent,
insight about the ri_... _. _....._....

And to my four close friends who agree that children have rights and
spent days of oral reading of this book with me, offering sage and
thoughtful advice.

*****

Cover design by Wingspan Graphics

Chapters (1 to 17)

Chapter One

Talkin' About A Revolution

The Genius Pirates

"What's the meaning of Life?"

That's the age-old question.

But it's not really the right question.

The better question is: "What's the meaning of YOUR life?"

Life is wonderful, but life is just life. We humans give our lives meaning by living, choosing, working, playing, loving – being what we can be, being all we can be. We choose what is meaningful for us. The meaning is not the same for everyone. It is highly individualistic. It is YOUR meaning. It is my meaning. It is the meaning that our children find and give to their lives.

Every morning when we get up, that day is the sum of everything we have put into our lives and made of our lives – our lovers, our friends, our belongings, our integrity, our honesty, our giving, our conversation, our commitments, our work, our children. Every morning, we begin to put new meaning into our lives with the free choices we make and the things we love to do.

But we can only have all those things and a meaningful life if we are FREE to make our own choices every day, if nobody is interfering with our lives and telling us what we must do or not do. When we get up in the morning, we must know that we have complete control over what we want to do with our lives that day – and every day.

Otherwise, what's the use? What's the meaning?

And so it is with our children, too. They need to be free every moment of their lives to choose what they want to do, so they can have their goals, their choices, their joy, their loves, their self-esteem, their satisfaction – their meaning. This doesn't become important when they turn 18. It becomes important the very moment they are born – and especially important the moment they begin to roam around our homes around the age of one and explore the things that are important to them in that moment of time. Each little free exploration has meaning to them.

If we parents stop free innocent discovery any time in our children's lives, we, unfortunately, interfere with their meaning – the same way we would lose meaning if we let those around us or the government interfere with our self-path.

Without their own meaningful discovery of life, kids will lack that full meaning. If a parent is running their life, even a little bit, then it won't be the child's meaning; it will be the parent's meaning, patched onto the child. When parents do this, kids cannot be fully happy with their own full meaningful discovery.

We parents should honor their right to the same self-determination we have, to let them create themselves completely new from infancy to adulthood. We must stand as their loving protectors, keeping them safe and ensuring that when they are seeking their goals and meaning that they don't walk on others – because those others have the same RIGHT to self-determination that our children have.

Many parents are very good and loving with their children, but they are not setting their kids fully free. Instead of allowing their kids complete freedom to choose and act, the parents are acting as unsolicited guides. They are using punishment or "rewards", talking sternly or showing impatience, pushing activities, nagging, making strong suggestions on what to do, giving ultimatums, restricting innocent actions, or forcing them into schools.

This book is about setting children completely and joyously free – and setting you free from some of the false constraints and ideas that have, unfortunately, been passed down through hundreds of generations and thousands of cultures.

Yes, we love our children deeply and would do anything for them. No doubt about that. But that isn't enough if we don't set them completely free as we remain the affectionate Watchman, to protect them and to stand strong when their freedom sometimes intrudes on others' freedom – or when others intrude on their freedom.

I will explain why kids have the right to be free – and how we parents handle a household in which all occupants, including our kids, are free to run their own lives and pursue their own meaning – without anyone stepping on toes.

Born To Be Wild – And Wise

Our children are born geniuses – baby Einsteins.

And they are born happy pirates – Jack Sparrows and Jackie Sparrows.

Genius pirates. That's a handful! They are quick. They are curious. They are information consumers on a grand scale. They bump up against their new world. (When I say "pirate", I mean of course the sense of adventure, not immorality.)

Their quest for knowledge and things in the first four years of their life is off the charts for us adults, who unfortunately don't remember that phase of our lives. It seems alien to those of us "old" people who have grown accustomed to the world.

But if you were shipwrecked on a strange island all by yourself, you'd immediately do what children do once they begin to walk: explore like crazy your new surroundings, cut things, build things, tear things down, scrounge for food, and find out as much as you could as quickly as you could.

That's a kid's life. The pirate life. This world is brand-spanking new and fascinating. They want to gobble it up. It is THEIR island.

When Bruce Springsteen was 15, he was riding in the car with his mom. Bob Dylan's song "Like a Rolling Stone" came on the radio. Later in life, Springsteen recounted the experience, saying, "On came that (opening) snare shot that sounded like somebody kicked open the door to your mind."

This is LIFE for children every day. Life is a snare-drum shot that kicks open the door to their minds – and they live it fully and experience it fully and joyfully. Frankly, this should be life for us adults too – a snare shot every day!

But within that "snare shot", they don't know "rights" boundaries at first? They don't even know there ARE boundaries or rights. They don't know that they have a right to "bump" and learn – as long as they let other people do the same. Their "gobbling up" sometimes takes them into others' snare shots, harming possessions, taking things, being too loud or hurting someone. They aren't being mean. They're just being curious pirates. They simply don't know they're bumping into others, until we tell them and explain to them and stand as firm as the oak tree in the front yard.

It's not our job to tame their wildness. We should revel in their glorious wild abandonment. But it is our job to ensure that their wild and wonderful experience of their world does not interfere with our experience or anyone else's experience.

That's our main job as parents – to ensure that their pirate adventure in this wonderful world is free and that they don't upset anyone else's pirate adventure. If we do this right, our love and affection and the relationship are pure and sweet and deep, without tension, anxiety or rebellion.

If our children are still "bumping" up against us and others between the ages of 4 and 18, that means we didn't quite honor their right to be free when they were younger – and we weren't an oak tree. They're restless from false restrictions. They have some inner anger left over from not being free, and they are "acting out". But there is absolutely no tension or residual anger in children who are raised to be free.

I talk in this book about how to get rid of that tension and anger by being what I call a Happy Oak Tree with kids you already have or kids you are about to have.

But, quickly, back to the newborns.

Our babies may not end up doing something as incredibly revolutionary as Albert Einstein or Marie Montessori, but their minds are revolutions in the making, ready to chart an exciting path to anywhere and everywhere.

In a way, I think they are a little more like Mozart, creating their own symphony out of life, instead of music.

They can rationally put things in their life together as well as young Mozart put music together. Their brains are wired to string facts together fast and efficiently, and the feelings they have about life are Mozartian. (Not "Martian". Ha!)

All of our lives should be symphonies of meaning – in which we play the main part and do all the conducting. Our kids should have the same kind of life and the same chance to conduct. Parents love them and take care of them, but parents sometimes get in the way of that conducting and think they know better what kids need.

They think they need to control their electronics use or the Internet or bedtimes or cleanliness or clothes or cussing or boyfriends and girlfriends or schooling or gaming or judgments or comments or "talking back" or friends or "sharing" or tree-climbing or hairstyle or tattoos or facial expressions or "no" or music or movies or sleepovers or eating or dinner times or silverware usage or nail-biting – etc.

Controlling these things or other things in our children's lives is suffocating – and gets in the way of them BEING somebody and creating themselves.

Unlike adults, children's symphonies are entirely new, as they learn how to use the most awesome instrument ever to exist: **the rational human mind**.

That mind is not just the greatest supercomputer to ever exist. It has something quite strange to our universe, something that no other animal has, something entirely new: **free will**. It can actually choose to go one way or another at any moment, either short term or long term, to learn and find meaning – as long as that free will is free from outside interference.

That mind can choose to be good or bad, to be lazy or productive, to be fair or not be fair, to do this thing and not do that thing, to make plans years in advance or live day-to-day like a lower animal – to be or not to be.

No other animal can choose to be or not to be. No other animal has a Hamlet. No other animal can CHOOSE. They are entirely instinctual, acting on stimuli only.

With that great mind and free will, our children are massively built for survival and information consumption and the pursuit of happiness.

But none of us can pursue our own happiness if we do not have control of where we are going in life – if someone else is calling the shots for us and telling us what to do. Us adults, you and me, have full individual rights – though the government does interfere somewhat with that, unfortunately. Many adults, especially women, feel the pressure of what others want us to do, but, in the end, we DO have the right to say, "Hell no, I'm not doing that. I'm going to do what I want to do. End of subject!"

Children should be able to say that, too.

Us adults can be proud of the things we do because we get to CHOOSE what we do all the time. To be happy, we have to be able to choose. Lucille Ball famously said:

"It's a helluva start, being able to recognize what makes you happy."

It took the gorgeous and funny redhead decades to figure out what truly makes her happy. She was not brought up as a free child. She didn't "start" being happy until she got a lot older, like most people. She wasn't raised with full rights. Our kids can "start" being happy and remain happy from the beginning.

Modern kids also aren't getting the same opportunity to be completely free and happy. They don't get to choose what they want to do all the time, even though their brains are just as big as ours (3 pounds) and they can learn just as fast as us adults (sometimes faster, it seems) and they are very good at what they do. They should be able to "start" as soon as they are born. They shouldn't have to wait, like lovely Lucy, for decades to start being happy and finally recognize what makes them happy.

This book is about changing the perception of kids and their wondrous minds. It is about taking our love of them to an even higher level than now, and honoring their right to not only co-exist, but also to the same self-direction and self-ownership that we have – the same self-ownership and independence that Lucy finally got.

This book is about a revolution in the way us parents think about our lovely pirates. It is about acknowledging their rights, thinking of them as friends first, talking to them as friends, making them equals in the home and outside the home, and learning how to handle this new revolutionary situation of being loving partners in life – instead of loving rulers.

It's very exciting and it CAN be done, with the right rules and principles in place. I'll talk a lot about those rules and principles. I'll talk a lot about what "rights" are and how there's only one primary rule for conduct when we all have rights: "You can do anything you want in life, as long as you don't trample on others while doing it." (Live and let live.)

This is the rule that our kids have the toughest time with in their first 8 years, but they do fully get it – as long as we are Happy Oak Trees.

Chapter Two

Born Free
The Kid Symphonies

When our kids' 3 pounds of raw brain power between their ears kicks in around one year old, they've got the mightiest thing in the known universe at their disposal. That is truly awe-inspiring.

They learn from one to five languages all by themselves by age four, depending on how many languages they are exposed to. (There are kids and adults in Europe who speak five to 10 languages. Incredible!)

They need absolutely no help from us parents to learn languages – though we do enjoy helping them. They learn them BY THEMSELVES simply by paying attention and wanting it. Wow, what a brain!

And yet, even after seeing this amazing feat, almost all parents think that kids somehow need to go to a "school" – to learn much easier things, like math or grammar or history or literature or geography or economics or whatever.

Language is tough to learn (as adults know when we try to learn a second language), and yet kids put together a vast array of concepts (words) relating to the outside world as if it were child's play. (Ahem) It IS child's play to them.

But schools actually slow our children down, and they implicitly tell children that they don't have the right to gather information themselves on their own time, as they did with language. Schools aren't designed primarily to impart information. They're designed to impart "direction" to little people who are currently in the process of finding their OWN direction, their own meaning. Schools are designed to impart obedience to others' directions. Schools violate our kids' rights to run their own lives and information-gathering.

In the U.S., there is a strong "unschooling" movement, in which children do not attend schools and have no curriculum. They are free to learn what they want when they want. My child was raised this way, too, and she is a voracious learner.

(In the U.S., there is also a strong movement called "free range" parenting, in which the parents don't helicopter their children and let them remain mostly free. I say "mostly" because the parents still do control some of the actions of the kids, including forcing them to go to school, among other things. The "free range" parents don't yet fully understand children's rights, but they are a vast improvement over most parenting around the world.)

But "rights" are not just about NOT forcing kids into schools away from home or even in the home. They're about NOT forcing them to do anything with their own lives that they don't want to do. Us parents don't have the right to force anyone, including our children and adult friends, to DO something. We only have the right to ensure that they DON'T do something against us or others – ensuring they understand that others have rights too.

This takes away a lot of the authoritative duties of being a parent in modern society, and isn't that a good thing? Do we really need to be running our children's lives – or ANYONE'S life, for that matter? No, we just need to be running our own lives and enjoying our own meaning – and of course enjoying our abiding relationship with our children.

Children remain symphonies, full of meaning, if we don't cause discord by interfering with their learning and conducting, by interfering with their path, by forcing them to learn what WE want them to learn, by forcing them to do things daily that WE want them to do.

Through the centuries, children have sensed something wrong with this "forcing" of them. They can't really put it into words until about age 8, but they know something is wrong. If kids are being forced to do things they shouldn't have to do (like wearing something they don't want to wear), they begin to rebel, and it usually starts around the age of 2. THIS is the reason for the clich of "The Terrible Twos", but it is brought on by parents, not kids. Kids raised free don't have terrible twos.

All human rebellion, from the beginning of civilizations, has been caused by this "forcing", by this violation of the human rights of kids. Rebellion begins in the home. Even the most loving of parents are startled by the rebellion, and they often think to themselves, "Well, kids are just that way at that age." But they don't have to be.

The children sense that they should be able to create their own symphonies, but even well-meaning parents insist on creating their own artificial symphonies for their children. They don't think the kids can conduct themselves. But they can.

Parents insist on being "in charge" and think that kids don't have the right to be in charge of themselves, so parents become the conductors, taking away the kids' own pursuit of happiness – which is necessary every single moment of our lives.

But children do have the same rights as adults from birth. The thing that gives them those rights is the same thing that gives parents their rights: the human mind, the rational mind, the volitional (free will) mind. There is no age qualification for rights. They either exist for all humans, or they don't exist at all.

THIS is the revolution!

The only primary difference between the parents and the kids is that the kids haven't YET gathered as much information as the parents have – but this is NOT a valid reason to negate the rights of children.

With kids having the same rights as us parents, the only thing us parents have to figure out is how to manage a household with the rights being equal. (That, in itself, is a revolution!) That is what I spend a lot of time explaining in this short book – after the primary thing, which is that kids have rights.

I explain how to set your children free and why they should be free – to be the awesome people they can be.

Solving the Problem of Millennia

For centuries, civilized people have denounced slavery – and to the credit of humans, it is now almost wiped out around the world.

For millennia, women were oppressed by the dominant chauvinism. Now, women's rights are recognized as the same as men's in civilized nations around the globe.

For thousands of years, those outside one's own group were considered inferior and "barbaric", but over the last century, that prejudice has changed dramatically.

But there is one group of people that remains enslaved or controlled or oppressed or "inferior" or not taken seriously enough – and there's hardly a word said about it. It's expected. It's even approved matter-of-factly.

These "inferior" people are children.

Even the very best of parents, unfortunately, treat their children with some condescension on occasion, falsely believing their kids need motivation or direction or reminding. Maybe it's hard to admit, but it's true. Though most parents obviously love their children, they really don't think their kids can figure out for themselves what they want or need to do. Sure the kids sometimes need help early on, but this is because of a lack of information. We can't be condescending towards people who simply haven't learned something yet, no matter their age.

If we are condescending towards our kids because they lack the knowledge and discipline we have, then we can't get angry at "elitists" we meet who perhaps have more knowledge and discipline than we have – and are condescending towards us, creating political correctness and governments that control us and our kids.

Some parents "helicopter" and control and punish and snipe and yell at kids almost as if the parents owned them.

Some parents "motivate" kids to do the things the PARENT wants them to do, falsely believing that children aren't motivated if left free.

Some parents love their kids and hug them in one moment, and in the next moment, take a "tone" with them that suggests that they are to do what the parent says – no questions asked – as if free people are to be addressed that way. We do not take tones with our friends, so why should we with our cherished children?

Some parents assume that since they birth their kids, the parents can do with them as they please. "They're mine and I'll raise them the way I want to!" Where is the child in that equation?

Some parents view children as "fallen", as if they were born with an evilness in their head – because they see kids do bad things or because their religions tell them this or both. But kids are born with no information or designs in them. They are cute little chubbies with their own tiny personalities in the crib, without any information or plans yet.

Children have, unfortunately, been raised badly since the dawn of civilization and therefore behaved badly, making people falsely believe that there must be something basically wrong with children – that they HAVE to be that way, and so they have to be controlled.

Some parents visit their bad moods on their kids – as if to say, "I'm in a bad mood and there's nothing you can do about it because you're in my control." If we try this same thing with our friends, we'll probably get a "bad mood" in return!

Many parents assume that kids will be terrible in their twos, rebellious in their teens, and some trouble 'tween – as if it simply has to be that way.

It doesn't. Free kids are not terrible ever. That probably sounds crazy to say, but it's true. Free kids get to do what they want with their lives, so they have no REASON to be terrible. They're not mad at anyone. It doesn't occur to them to rebel. There's nothing to rebel against. They are no trouble because nobody is causing them trouble by telling them what to do all the time.

Peter Gray, Ph.D., a professor in the Department of Psychology at Boston College, has this to say about parents' acting on the false belief that kids will allegedly be bad and need to be controlled by parents:

"Sadly, in many cases, the assumption that children are incompetent, irresponsible, and in need of constant direction and supervision becomes a self-fulfilling prophecy. The children themselves become convinced of their incompetence and irresponsibility, and may act accordingly. The surest way to foster any trait in a person is to treat that person as if he or she already has it."

Some loving parents unconsciously visit this "assumption" daily upon their children, telling their kids when to eat, what to eat, when to go to bed, when to brush their teeth, when to talk, who to date, when to get home at night, what to buy, what to wear, when they can drive, whom to associate with, when to wash their hands, or even when to cross a street, when they are plenty old enough to know themselves.

My daughter and I saw this assumption just the other day. A mom was with her three kids, ages 10 to 13, and she warned them of "traffic" before they crossed a street. The kids, of course, gave her a look like "duh" but didn't dare say anything. That kind of helicoptering by the mom does not show that she cares, though she probably thinks it does. It shows that she doesn't trust her kids' minds to handle something simple. If she'd seen the wry looks on her kids' faces and the rolling of eyes, she would've known how they REALLY took her nagging. It wasn't good.

Parents tell kids they must go to school, must not watch too much TV, must not cuss, must do their homework, must not play too many video games, must wear certain clothes, must not walk around naked at home, must share THEIR belongings, must not "talk back", must respect their elders, must not judge others, must take baths or showers, must do things for others … and so on.

Even the best of parents "suggest" some of the above. In polite circles, it's called nagging. But it implies to the kids the same negative thing: We don't totally trust their abilities and we think they don't have a right to do as they please with their own bodies and their own things. Though a parent may see this as their way of showing love, it is never taken that way by kids, and the kids are right. They know the parent is trying to run their lives. They may be obedient when told to do these things, but the rebellion underneath is beginning and swelling – and it WILL come out sooner or later in various ways, and greatly upset the parents, who believed they were doing the right things when helicoptering.

It's little wonder, isn't it, that children rebel? I know that I did as a youth, starting very early, as did all my friends. My friends and I were constantly told some or all of the above. One minute our parents were kissing us, and the next minute they were either nagging or demanding. It sends mixed signals. When my friends and I were about 12, I remember one of them saying, "Why don't my parents trust me?!" Yep!

Many parents do love their kids and are well-meaning, but they inadvertently promote this rebellion by not honoring their kids' right to run their own lives – and living with the consequences, good and bad.

In the EXTREME, it's been horrible parenting that created all the turmoil of the world among the adults we meet every day, whether it is in homes or out in society.

Throughout history, all the problems of the world have been caused by horrible parenting – wars, poverty, depression, hostility, murder, robbery, brutality, obesity, lying, irresponsibility, laziness, apathy, destruction, deceit, terrorism, abuse, bullying, injustice, road rage, gangs, addiction, cheating, teen-age rebellion, low self-esteem. It may have been bad philosophies or religions or cultural ideas that spurred the parents, but it was, in the end, the PARENTS who were horrible.

All of this sounds terrible and maybe even improbable to many of you. But I will explain later how kids' not having control of their lives and having low self-esteem can go on terrible, destructive paths. All of us have thought or even said, "What kind of childhood did those people have?!"

This book is the answer to that question.

Please don't think that I am talking about you, the loving parent who is reading this book, when I say "horrible" parenting throughout history. But the point does need to be made about very bad parents, so that we have perspective about what goes on in the world.

It would be very difficult to "fix" these horrible parents, but this book is not about horrible parents. It is about loving, caring parents who want to take their love and caring to the next level by honoring their kids' natural rights to exist and run their lives. It is a wonderful journey of friendship and abiding trust.

Chapter Three

The Happy Oak Tree
The Confident Care-Friend With THE Solid Rule

There is just one essential fix for all of us parents who want to raise happy, thoughtful, independent kids. Here it is:

We acknowledge that children have full-blown individual rights.

Total equality with us adults.

It takes a different way of viewing kids' minds, their abilities, parenting, and even life itself to get to that acknowledgment. In the last chapter, I address what parents can do to better prepare themselves for life's daily challenges and opportunities. Though many parents can be objective and fair, it takes TOTAL fairness and objectivity to be not just a great person, but also a great person to our children. It is vital – not just for our kids, but mainly for us.

So, what does it mean that children have rights and we parents have rights?

It means we both can and cannot do things. We can do things with our own lives, but can't trounce on others while doing it, because they've got the same rights.

I'm sure you noticed it's the same rule we have with other adults, but because kids have been seen as the virtual property of their parents, that same right has never been extended to kids. As far as I'm aware, there's never even been an explanation of why kids don't have the same rights, which suggests the depth to which people believe they don't have them.

So what are rights? They are, essentially, a protection from other people's actions against us without provocation. They are a restriction on how far we can go with our pursuits while around others and their property. As the saying goes, "Your rights end where my nose begins." (I explain this in detail in Chapter Seven.)

So, with children, that means they also get to do whatever they want, just like us, every day – and the only thing they can't do is violate other people's space, time, property and body – inside the home and out in society. That is their PRIMARY rule they must follow, like us. Really, it's the ONLY rule. All other rules branch off of the rule of honoring others' rights.

And our primary job in raising them is to ensure that we are their Happy Oak Tree (It's a corny metaphor, I know, but I like it because oak trees are majestic, gorgeous and hard – like real life.). We are the oak tree of reality who ensures that our kids understand and follow the one primary rule of conduct concerning not violating others' rights.

When I say "Happy Oak Tree", I don't mean we walk around with a silly grin on our face. (LOL) I mean that our watchfulness and explanation of the rights of all members of a family are as solid as an oak tree in the front yard, and that we are comfortable and happy with our job as the oak tree. We are happily resolute.

The reality of our gentle firmness is just as real as the mighty tree. It means we are content in being the Oak Tree and are not being mean when we put our foot down. Kids need this; they want this; they get this; they thrive off of objective rules of conduct towards others; they eventually enforce these rules themselves as little oak trees around others. But the rules have to be perfectly right, based only on the primary rule of not messing with others while pursuing happiness. If we are off on our fairness just a little bit, it will backfire with rebellion and disrespect from them.

As Happy Oak Trees, we become benevolent boundaries for our kids' errant actions and errant Paths until they learn for themselves how to act without harming others.

I'll be explaining how new parents or soon-to-be parents can be Happy Oak Trees and honor their kids' rights from the beginning and ensure happiness throughout the parent/child experience. And then I'll explain how those with older children can "fix" their relationships by becoming the Oak Tree and using "Leverage" (the things you own) benevolently but firmly. It can be done!

From Parents to Care-Friends

Though I'm a parent of a lovely daughter, I've never really liked how the term "parent" was used – as the person in charge of the child. Yes, I'm a parent in the sense of happily being my daughter's loving care-taker – but I've always felt more friend than parent. I enjoy having fun with her and helping her, just like my best adult friends. I've also found it interesting that since she was 6 years old, she occasionally calls me by my first name, which I assume means that she sees me as an equal – which I enjoy, but I know some parents bristle at the thought.

When my spouse and I were talking about having a baby, I realized I wanted to have the baby so that I could have another great friend – a trusting, loving, adoring friend who would need my caring for a good while. I'd been told that your children shouldn't be your friends, but I think it's just the opposite. I think the goal of any would-be parent should be to have kids in order to have more bosom buddies.

After deciding I wanted a friendship with my child, I decided I wanted to think of myself as something more than a parent, so the name "Care-Friend" popped to mind. I know. Makes you think of "Care-Bear". Sounds corny, but, hey, when you're talking about children, you have a right to be corny!

Because I've thought of myself as a friend, or Care-Friend, it has acted as a constant reminder of what kind of relationship I'm trying to build, of the value of my child, of the fact that she has rights to be treated like an adult friend, with her freedom intact.

When I'm the Oak Tree, I do it as a Care-Friend, being sure that I'm being fair and that I'm explaining myself very well and thoughtfully – and that I'm treating her as the equal person she has a right to be.

As Care-Friends, we should communicate to our kids what we are feeling, what we are thinking, what we are judging, what we know, what we want, what we like – exactly as we do with our close adult friends, with passion, kindness, firmness and respect. We share our lives fully with them, the good and the bad. Kids LOVE this, and respect us more when we fully communicate and respect their ability to handle virtually anything. If we do not communicate fully with children, they will not respect or trust us. It shows we're holding back something.

Once our kids' minds kick into nearly full gear around the age of two, we should address them exactly as we do our closest adult friends, in the exact same tone (no baby-talk), acknowledging their rights to their own opinions and actions – ensuring that their actions and our actions don't interfere with one another's life, property, money and space.

We change from being rulers of our children to benevolent oak trees and friends – alert to our children's safety and always ensuring that their rights are honored by everyone as we travel down our life-paths together.

The Path of Least Resistance

One of the keys to "getting" children and relating to them well is understanding how we all propel though life – about the Path of Least Resistance. Like kids, when we adults want something, we take the shortest path possible to get it, whether it's a new car, or a piece of chocolate, or a boyfriend/girlfriend, a new job, a clean house, new music, new phone, something across the room, a fit body, a cup of coffee, a restaurant, jewelry, a friendship, a new home.

Kids are the pirates of pleasure and acquisition. They've got a new island world in front of them and they want absolutely everything they can get their hands on and they want it NOW – which means that their Path of Least Resistance is like Occam's Razor, full-steam straight ahead. If we adults are not Happy Oak Trees when our kids' paths run over others, then we will end up with brats and bullies. More on that later.

In our adult Path of Least Resistance, we gather information as fast as we can (often through the Internet and friends) to get our cars, phones, music, homes, mates. We go directly to the chocolate at the store, unless there's someone in our path in the aisle, and then we go around them politely. If we try to bump them out of the way (like a young child might do), we not only violate their right to their body, but we also create the potential for a showdown, thereby wasting time and turning the least-resistant path into the most-resistant path.

Us good adults have discovered that the Path of Least Resistance is often a parabola or circle path, so that we don't harm others and their paths – so that we save time and respect their rights and hope that they will do the same for us.

For instance, once we've gathered enough information on homes, we go on tours of homes. If the Realtor is with another couple, then we quietly wait our turn to see the home, so we don't create resistance, and so that we honor the other couple's rights.

With boyfriends and girlfriends, we think about what we want in them and then go out with those who seem to fit the profile, so we don't waste time. Wasting time is a bad path full of resistance.

In each of the above scenarios, we took the Path of Least Resistance. If you didn't do your research on cars and phones and music and a home, you might pick the wrong one and then have to return it or just have to live with it – creating a lot of resistance (time-wasting stress) in your life that could've been avoided, creating unhappiness.

If you rudely interrupt the Realtor at the home, she will not be happy with you and therefore may not tell you the truth about the home or everything good about the home or get you to buy a home you really don't want, thereby creating more resistance in your path, reducing your happiness. You know this, but young kids often don't understand that what seems like the shortest Path might end up being the longest Path. So, as the Happy Oak Tree, we communicate with them and teach them these things in what I call the Lightning Moments of parenting.

Each Lightning Moment MUST be addressed as quickly and firmly and nicely as possible. Any hesitation on your part shows weakness, which kids are geniuses at picking up on.

Like us adults, kids eventually learn that the shortest path is not always the direct path. They will follow your Oak Tree example, understanding that we can't run over other people's rights (bodies, property, time and money) while getting to our exciting destination. They honor other people's rights, and in doing so, they end up avoiding resistance.

At a family reunion or dinner party or business gathering, many of us adults avoid those we don't like, because they create resistance to our happiness. Avoiding eye contact with unpleasant people is the Path of Least Resistance. (I do it a lot! Gawd, some people!)

Some rude adults attempt to go down what they think is a Path of Least Resistance, in which they walk through the lady in the grocery store aisle or rudely interrupt the Realtor or steal music and movies off the Internet, knowing that they haven't paid a dime for them.

In each case, they've imposed on others or outright violated their rights, often creating more resistance on their paths because the lady at the store protests and stalls their progress or the Realtor lies to them because they disrespected her and her protocol or because they end up in jail for the theft.

Rude people run over others and end up creating more resistance, though they expect all of the above people to be wallflowers who won't protest, like wallflower parents. These rude people create cognitive dissonance (mental confusion) in their own minds because of their horrible conduct. Deep down, they know they are acting badly. The resulting loss of self-esteem creates a resistance to happiness.

Young children often don't mean to be "bad" or rude, but they will often go down the same paths that impose on others because the kids don't understand yet what rights are and that others must sometimes be taken into account along the Path – until the Oak Tree explains things over and over and over. Older kids who are rude to parents and others have found that their Path of Least Resistance is simply to run over weak people who won't protest, thereby allowing the older child to get what they want. These older children, unfortunately, don't have Happy Oak Trees in their lives.

Until about the age of 4, kids generally aren't being purposely mean. They aren't quite that smart yet. And they certainly weren't born evil. They may try to "get away" with things, but they're doing it because they want something badly. They're simply on a hunt for survival, acquisition and fun. Their Path is full-steam ahead. That is a great thing, as long as they understand the primary rule of honoring others' rights. They eventually get it.

The Happy Oak Tree is essential for this critical stage. If the kids get a basic understanding of the limits that rights entail at this age, your Oak Tree job afterward is pretty darn easy, with rare flare-ups – much like adult friends, actually.

I will talk in a later chapter about how to carefully use your Leverage (the things you own) to ensure that you get their attention on the boundaries of rights.

If we haven't done our Oak Tree job very well in those first four years, the child's Path of Least Resistance runs right through US as the years go by. They will simply trample over us and others to get what they want. Throwing a tantrum or getting loud in a restaurant or lying or taking our belongings or destroying things becomes the easy (non-resistant) path to getting their way.

Or worse. They might become obedient young drones who do as they are told. This, unfortunately, is all too common – it stunts their free will and personal motivation. Many parents cherish obedience and think it's a very good quality. They think it makes it easier on their parenting. But it's actually the sign of surrender, of worrying about what others want, of not following their own Path to happiness, of living by rules that don't make much sense. It is the beginning of the end of individuality.

It is Paths of Least Resistance gone bad that has caused all the bad behavior in history, and it is, unfortunately, this bad behavior that has led most adults throughout history to erroneously believe that children are simply born bad – born "fallen". But it is bad Paths, not bad brains, that is the real problem, and it can be fixed by Happy Oak Trees.

All of us have had friends or even lovers whom we felt like we had to "babysit" occasionally. These people did not have Oak Trees in their lives. If we've been the Happy Oak tree with our kids, we won't have to babysit much at all by the time they are four years old. They GET it.

If we are an Oak Tree with kids, they soon realize and respect the fact that we cause them way too much resistance for their intended bad purposes. They learn to properly honor us and others while they pursue what they want and need. They eventually learn to respect us and others for who we are as they fly down their pirate Paths of Least Resistance.

Chapter Four

Being Self-Full
Parents and Kids Must Be Free to Have Self-Fulfillment

Honoring this new relationship of rights is all about our kids and US. It is about OUR self-fulfillment and THEIR self-fulfillment in the home and in our happiness-pursuits together. It is about both of us being "self-full" – fulfilling the needs of our complex self in an environment where all people are freely trying to do the same.

This idea about fulfilling one's self amidst others in a home and billions of others on planet Earth is the only reason why we have the concept of "rights". Nobody needs or has rights if they are alone on an island. There is no one else to interfere with your Path of Least Resistance. It is only when another person comes to your island that you have rights and that they must be honored by the other person. "Rights" is concept that refers only to life around other people. We don't have rights when we are alone on an island or around the lower animals, who cannot honor rights. It is a concept that limits our actions in society.

Virtually all of the readers of this book agree with the above statement about rights, and yet most of you don't think that children could possible have the exact same rights and that, if they did, it would most likely turn a household into mayhem.

It doesn't. In fact, it's quite the opposite. It is a peaceful, fun household of mutual respect and enjoyment. A free kid eventually becomes a responsible, self-full kid.

Because this idea of treating kids as complete equals is still off-putting to many of you, I hope it becomes clear how well it plays out as the book progresses – how both Care-Friend and child remain self-fulfilled (self-full).

A Brief Trip Down the Rabbit Hole

But, briefly, let's talk about a few of the nightmare situations that may have just run threw your brain from the thought of children having complete individual rights – like you've just spun down the rabbit hole. Here are a few thoughts:

1) "But they will run over everybody in the house." – No, you are the Oak Tree who has a tight bond with them and loves them and interacts with them and puts your foot down firmly and fairly whenever they violate others' rights. The kids are free, but they HAVE to honor others' rights to the same freedom. They get this real fast at a very early age if you stay on your game. As long as they feel your communication and feel your great love for them and their rights, they will always pay attention when you are the Oak Tree.

2) "But they will simply play games all day and do nothing else." – Maybe, maybe not. I know that I sometimes do ("Words With Friends"!). Just like adults, children have their "obsessions" for a while and the obsessions may last for a day or a week or a month or six months or longer, but they move on, just like we do when we're bored with something or learned everything we want to learn from it – unless it is something that may be a life-choice for kids, and then they keep doing it off and on, just like we do.

3) "But they will be unmotivated and do nothing." – I've yet to see such a thing as an unmotivated child who has been raised free. They are remarkably motivated ALL THE TIME. What curbs motivation is helicopter parenting and unfair parenting, with the child feeling like their life is not in their control and they are waiting to be told what to do. Their free will is evaporating. They stop thinking about what they want to do with their lives and start thinking about what others want them to do with their lives. This is what causes laziness and second-handedness, worrying about what others think.

4) "But if they have total rights, then I can't tell them what to do!" – Yep, that's it in a nutshell! And they can't tell YOU what to do. Works both ways. This is one of the keys to understanding children. They always know what they want to do, even if it's doing nothing (chilling) for a while, like us adults. Once you tap into them like you do a best friend, you get this. If we do have an issue with the actions of our children and they won't listen, that's when we firmly and fairly use our Oak Tree Leverage to change the behavior (the Path).

5) "But they will get a big head if they know they are free to do anything, and they will take advantage of this and be spoiled."

– Do you have a big head because you are free? (Ha!) No, and neither do free kids. They expect nothing more than their freedom. A spoiled child is a child whose whims and tantrums are accommodated by weak parents, who aren't oak trees. They are "given" things to shut up. They run down their Paths willy-nilly. They learn to use and abuse the weak household system. A free child is just the opposite. They learn from your Happy Oak Tree responses that you will not allow any action that harms others or tries to take advantage of others. Children actually WANT to be treated this way because they seek a family environment that is just as clearly delineated as the oak tree in the front yard. It is hard and fast, and it does not change. It gives them comfort. It keeps them from being spoiled. Freedom didn't give America's Founders a big head or you and I big heads, and it certainly doesn't give children big heads.

6) "But what if they don't want to learn anything." – As former longtime educator John Holt once said, "Humans are the learning animal." We are constantly learning, and children are the specialists, learning more than 100 new things a day from ages 1 through 10. Their spectacular 3-pound brains are WIRED to learn at a breath-taking pace. They LIKE to learn. By the age of 10, they can learn – by themselves – enough information to handle 90% of the jobs on Earth, even though that wasn't their goal. They may not seem like they are learning when, for example, they are playing video games, but even then they are learning cooperation, dexterity, strategy, math, spelling, handling other people, communication, diplomacy, that losing is a natural part of life and makes you stronger, etc. This goes for everything from sports to dressing dolls to building plastic armies to searching the Internet to chess to cartoon-watching and much more. If you want to form that everlasting trust-bond with your children, join them happily in some of these moments – after ASKING them for their permission to do so. You only ask permission from people who have the authority to grant you permission, and children have that authority, just like we do. But the most important aspect of this question is that it is really none of our business what and when our children are learning. I don't mean that in a mean way. I just mean that what our friends learn and when they learn it isn't our decision or, really, our business. We are interested and love to hear about it, yes, but when it comes down to it, it is THEIR business. We would love to help them learn, if they ask. But, they have the right to learn what and when they wish, just like we do. We are always curious what they're learning, but if it enters your head that you

are worried about what they are learning, then you have now gone over to the "control" side of parenting.

I'm writing this book for those who love their children but who are consciously or subconsciously not quite honoring their full rights to run themselves. They are possibly treating them as inferiors, whose lives must be monitored and arranged and run to some small or large degree, and possibly buying into the historical view that children are not really full people yet.

How we treat our children will be their history when they become adults. As Shakespeare said, "Past is prologue." How we VIEW our children is their prologue to their adulthood epilogue. They will largely act and feel about themselves according to how we treat them now. If they feel like they are free, they will act free. They will be self-full. If they don't feel like they are free, they will never expect it, and their "self" will suffer.

How we treat our children also says a lot about us. Do we think their growing minds are capable or not capable? Should it be controlled by others or set free to blossom? When it comes down to it, are we "controllers" or "liberators" of our children? Let's be liberators!

If we view children as under our control or under our "ownership", they will feel that condescension and "act out" their frustration at not being able to control themselves, no matter how good we attempt to make their surroundings and no matter how much we love them. They WILL do bad things, whether small or big, to themselves and to others. They will become "other" oriented for their direction in life, constantly fretting over what other people think, and worrying about being judged – instead of being their own best guide and judge always.

But when rights are honored, there is no such thing as dysfunction. Only function. Both the parents and the children are self-full and have high self-esteem from being able to run their own lives. True self-esteem is the result of having the overall assessment of yourself as capable.

A good way to think about children is this: "They've got awesome brains, and they just have to gather a lot of facts about life and figure some things out, and I'm going to help make sure they're safe until they can figure it all out, and I'm going to love them and talk with them about what's right and wrong, and we'll do this thing together".

After all, you're trying to create a best friend forever (I know, I just BFF'd!).

BFF

We can't be equals with a friend we feel superior to. Many of us have tried that before, and it just doesn't work out in the long-term. And that goes for children too. If we don't see them as people with rights that are equal to ours and as people who will soon be as equally capable as us, it's a recipe for disaster.

We must see them as our growing friends – our growing BEST friends.

Even though they start out small and ignorant and make many mistakes along the way, we should still treat them as dear friends. Dr. Seuss once said: "A person's a person – no matter how small."

Yes!

If infants could talk when they were born and knew what was about to go down in a long life, they might say something like this to you: "Hey, great to meet you. Please just do for me what I would do for myself for about 10 or so years, and I'll take it from there, outside of needing some cash and love and friendship and transportation PLEASE. Thanks very much!"

In other words, "Please take care of me, stay strong and loving, talk with me a lot, play with me, and let me just explore this universe until I figure things out myself."

We have to do those five things if we care for them – and if we want our kids to respect us and pay attention to us. But our kids don't HAVE to respect us. We have to earn it, just like with an adult friend – by treating them as equals. There should be no "respecting of elders" in life. There should only be respecting of people who run their lives well and let others run their lives – of people who are self-full.

The ONLY primary difference between kids and adults is knowledge. That's it. Our temporarily superior knowledge-base does not give us the right to run their lives in any way, shape or form.

Also, giving birth to children does not imbue some magical ownership on us parents. Yes, our kids are definitely part of our family, by law, but we don't get to say, "Alright, you're mine, and you'll be what I want you to be, and you're a part of this family I'm starting, so I get to at least partially make you into what I want. Oh, and I'm going to show you off to other people, as long as you do what I say."

Honoring kids' rights keeps us all self-full – and we never have to take trips down rabbit holes, except when we really ARE going down rabbit holes of adventure!

Whole New Perspective

Parents have been doing many standard things for centuries that they thought would be good for their kids. But, unfortunately, they are usually condescending-type of things. Like these:

1) The raised eyebrow of scorn
2) The insistence on schooling or sports, whether the child wants to or not
3) Bed times
4) The controlling of what the child wears or how they wear it
5) The "trophy" attitude of having the "honors" child (bumper stickers!)
6) Exasperation comments like "Do you REALLY have to do that?"
7) "Motivation" talks like "Why don't you do that? You're good at it."
8) Control moments – "You could use a haircut. You're watching a lot of TV. You're playing a lot of games. Why don't you like vegetables? You should share. Haven't you gotten ready YET? Why don't you have your shoes on yet? Why can't you get out of the car fast, like other people? Why do you always (fill in the blank). You should respect your elders. What are you doing on the Internet? You need to smile more. I know you don't like your cousins, but this is a family reunion, so can't you just go talk to them? Candy is bad for your teeth. Laughing at others is rude. Why can't you be like your sister?!"
9) "Because I said so!" (Really? Would we say that to our friends?!)
10) "Hurry up"

A more subtle form of condescension is NOT expecting children to do what they are truly supposed to do and CAN do. For example:

1) Continually cleaning their dishes or messes for them after the age of four, when they are old enough to do so

29

2) Not explaining to them the necessity of apologies and responsibility
3) They won't do good things because kids are just bad deep down
4) Letting the child interfere with others' spaces via noise or unruliness
5) Getting things for the child repeatedly when the child could get those things
6) Letting them cheat a little on games and sports, so they allegedly won't feel "hurt" or "bad" – or so they won't throw a fit
7) Letting them "win" games when they haven't won or couldn't win. (I never let my daughter win at games, but when she finally starting beating me at things like Monopoly and Twister and Foosball, she was positively giddy and knew that she earned it. Her pride was off the charts.)
8) Praising them too highly to make them allegedly feel better
9) Offering them rewards for "good conduct" – as if good conduct wasn't itself a reward for all of us. We don't offer our friends rewards for good conduct. In fact, we don't even use the phrase "good conduct" with them
10) Taking crap from them when you don't deserve crap
11) Asking them not to judge others because they might mess up on their judgment or because YOU feel uncomfortable about it

The extreme case of the first form of condescension above creates a rebel. The extreme case of the second form creates the spoiled brat. Most children (and "adults") throughout history have been somewhere in between severe brat or rebel.

But if we have the EXPECTATION of them being our friends, it prevents condescending behavior by us and creates responsibility in them: no brats or rebels.

Most parents feel some love or a lot of love for their children, but it is almost always mixed with some form of coercion or intimidation or threats or punishment or mind games or "motivation" or other forms of manipulation of them or their environment – suggesting that we don't trust them and implying that they can't and shouldn't run their own lives and don't have a right to.

This short book is about getting rid of all those bad things by fully understanding that Children Have Rights, that children should be our valued partners and friends throughout life, and that children are NOT primarily children.

They are primarily people! Secondarily, they are children.

That's a bit cutesy, admittedly, but it's a whole new perspective on how to view children – as little adults in the making.

And it all starts right in our homes. If we have a child who grows up with the full power and self-esteem that comes with their rights being honored, they can do anything in life and always take responsibility for their own lives.

Recognizing children's rights won't just set them free – it will set YOU free and make you even more self-full. You'll have no more bad thoughts about your child, no more hurt feelings, no more regret, no more anxiety, no more irritation, no more worry about what they'll do around the house or in public or with their boyfriends or girlfriends, no more concern about them being able to handle themselves and their future. They will be happily responsible and independent – and leave you free to enjoy them and your own life.

What you'll be able to see is a blossoming young human being in full charge of their lives, with full respect for your being lovingly with them through the journey.

I will explain in detail in the later chapters how we as parents can integrate the rights of children into our daily lives without even an iota of disruption or residual anger between the parties for the ENTIRETY of the relationship.

Sound too good to be true? … It's not.

Hope you'll come along for this short ride into child-parent respect and friendship – and how everyone in the family becomes entirely self-full!

But first, a quick fictional story about a woman named Claire.

Chapter Five

Claire
The Spider Inside Her

You and your soulmate are walking in the woods behind your home. She's bitten by a colorful, exotic spider. One hour later, she's woozy. Two hours later, she's almost delirious.

At the hospital, she falls into a coma. The doctors ask you to describe clearly what the spider looked like. It takes the doctors 24 hours to pinpoint the spider and the illness. She was bitten by a rare African spider. The implications are horrifying, say the doctors. After looking at cases in Africa, they give the following prognosis:

Claire, 30 years old, will be in a coma or semi-comatose state for the next year.

Starting in Year 2, she'll come completely out of her semi-comatose state and be fully conscious and wobbly, but she'll have full-blown amnesia and not even remember anything she ever learned, including language, and she'll have to learn everything all over again. She'll be foggy at first, but her rational mind will begin kicking in again a little at a time. She'll be able to perceive things and make some causal connections and begin rudimentary speaking. But she'll often harm herself while doing things. She'll have to be watched and helped a lot.

From the third to fifth year, she'll begin to really understand things around her and start talking fluently, but she'll have a bit of a difficult time adjusting to the world and learning the rules.

From year 6 through 10, Claire will learn how to read, do math, digest complex concepts, and she will get back almost entirely to where she was when she was bitten, with rare occasions of still grappling with honesty, justice, and integrity until about the 12th year – at which time, she should be fully back to her vital former self.

You and Claire had planned for potential catastrophic occurrences before the spider bite, but neither of you could've imagined such a horrendous state.

You grapple with your values, but you decide, yes, you will care for her during those 12 years, being her caretaker, changing her diapers at first, stopping her from harmful acts, being her helper through this wonderful life, chatting with her often, lengthily explaining complex matters when she's ready and willing – and honoring her right to govern and run her own life.

Children Are Like Claire

As I'm sure many of you figured out already, Claire's story is essentially that of a child in her first 12 years: complete incapacitation as an infant to near full mental growth and morality by age 12. Claire essentially became an infant again and had to start life over, brand new.

I think we can all agree that Claire obviously would not and did not surrender her individual rights when she was bitten by the spider and lost her identity – even though she essentially reverted to an infant state. But she needed a Care-Friend, an Oak Tree, which is what her soulmate became while Claire struggled down her Paths of Least Resistance towards the things she wanted.

Our children also don't surrender their rights as infants. They are smaller and younger than Claire, yes, but those are the only significant differences between the two – and those differences don't mean that kids suddenly don't get the same opportunity and have the same right of self-direction that Claire had. If we say that Claire kept her rights when she reverted to an infant stage, can't we say that infants have the same rights?

Few of you reading that story believed that Claire had lost her rights because of the tragic bite and her reversal to infancy, and yet nearly every adult throughout history has thought that children don't have the same rights – that they need to be treated like "children", that we somehow "own" them or can simply tell them what to do, as if they had no say in the matter and their life was ours.

Frankly, this "ownership" has GOT to change.

This is a crucial point. The only primary differences between children and Claire are age and size. Claire gets treated with automatic respect for her choices as she moves forward because she is "older" and bigger, and children do not because they are tiny and "new".

Claire had a Care-Friend – someone who would never consider that Claire lost any rights and who would take care of her with the utmost respect, even when she was "losing it". THIS is how children should be treated – with complete respect, as if they were Claire. It was easier for Claire's soulmate to treat her with respect because they had a "history". But we begin creating our history with our children the moment they are born.

What will that history be?

Children should be our soulmates, our bosom buddies – and we should treat them that way all the time!

If what happened to Claire happened to your best friend right now, would you treat them as if they had rights? Yes, you would. So would I. You would not dream of telling them what they must do all the time. You would not dream of telling her she must brush her teeth and go to school. You would try to reason with her and be kind to her and help her through her first period of life.

Claire's soulmate will keep her healthy, stop her from taking action against herself (even with temporary force if Claire is about to harm herself), and provide a moral and robust environment for mental growth. Her soulmate will be a Happy Oak Tree if she attempts a bad Path of Least Resistance and gently but firmly show her the right direction for mutual trust and respect.

If she chooses not to go to a formalized school, her soulmate would not THINK to try to make her go. If she chooses to watch video games for three months, she would. If she chooses late bedtimes, so be it.

Children have those same individual rights. Their "smallness" and "babbling" and harmful value pursuits (running into street) do not make them inferior, nor do they mean a surrender of rights, and nor do they mean that they are somebody's property. They just mean that they have some learning to do. And we are there as their loving Oak Tree and help them till they can stand on their own two feet mentally, so to speak.

Dr. Seuss: "A person's a person, no matter how small."

The caretaker status that children are in from birth does not assign authoritarian privilege to us caretakers. The only right we Care-Friends have that no other outside adults have is the right to BE the caretaker of our child. They are our children to protect and help when they need it. But they are not clay for us to mold. They mold themselves and conduct their symphonies on their own time schedules. And they are quite good at it, if left to their own devices as our friends.

34

Seeing our kids as friends with full rights puts the context of the relationship in clear Care-Friend focus – and prevents us adults from adopting a better-than-thou attitude or ownership attitude. We are there to do for them what they can't yet do for themselves.

Let's expand on that conversation that a child might have with a parent at birth:

"Hey. Howdy. Good to finally see some good lighting. Look, I'm going to need you to please take care of me for a good bit, keep me from doing harmful stuff, clean me up, give me some tasty, nutritious food (that umbilical was getting OLD), and, well, you know the rest. I hope to love you one day, and I know you wouldn't have gone through all this if you didn't think I'd be pretty cool too. I'll be calling you mommy and daddy soon. Please be patient. I got a whole heck of a lot of things in this exciting world I'm gonna want to learn and do. I hope you'll honor my right to pursue those things totally. I'll eventually learn to honor yours, too. I'll be a bit boring sometimes because you've already been through a lot of the cool stuff. And I'll be a bit, um, difficult sometimes till I figure out the right rules, with your help. Stay strong. Just explain them to me and stay strong. I'll come around eventually and be a lot of fun. Thanks a lot. I'm hungry. Where's the boob? Talk to you later."

All children are that kid who just spoke. All children are "Claire."

Her soulmate would never think of spanking her or hitting her or talking down to her or telling her what to do with her life or scolding her or being condescending to her.

He would honor her. He would honor her right of self-direction, and when she was "acting like a child," he would gently and rationally help her with explanations – sometimes possibly for hours, until she figured it out. He would use his Leverage if necessary. He would use his natural curiosity about the world to begin conversations with her and enjoy the moment.

He would love her, and he would look forward to loving her more, and he would hope that she would love him for his gentleness, his firmness, his values, his morality, his forthrightness – for who he is.

He knows he is her protection proxy for a while and he welcomes it.

After the spider attack, Claire started with nothing, a blank slate in her head: no information, no identity, no memories, no attached feelings toward anything. A blank slate, just like infants.

Outside of nipple radar, infants are like Claire: starting with nothing but a mental capacity (rationality). Then they slowly learn to run it, practice with it, use it well, be happy.

They are completely unaware of the extraordinary 3-pound thing between their ears. They have no idea what kind of power they have to run their universe.

Let's talk briefly about that extraordinary thing between our children's ears. It's the key to everything! I think that sometimes we take it for granted – in ourselves and in our kids.

Let's talk about Claire 30 years ago, when she was born.

Chapter Six

The Brain Child
The Three Pounds That Moves the World

In the beginning …

One of the ironies of being human and being far greater than other animals is that we are arguably the most helpless when we are born, entirely dependent on our mother primarily in the beginning.

About 5 million years ago, proto-humans had brains about the size of chimps, but now Claire is born with three times the brain size and a million times the computing power. If you've seen those old videos of the giant IBM computers filling entire rooms at NASA, Claire has that beat hands-down – all kids do.

A HUGE brain!

In one of those seemingly ironic twists of evolution, nature ended up making the brain of humans so big that the head couldn't fit through the mom's birth canal, so the baby effectively had to be born "early" and BEFORE the brain was finished developing – making young Claire the only animal that is incapable of any kind of self-survival for years and not even able to grasp her surroundings for months.

But THEN …

But then that 3-pound brain develops – and speeds past even the higher animals like a rocket zooming past a wagon.

In a few years, her extraordinary brain will have 100 trillion synapses and be capable of lightning fast conceptions and deductions, with the ability to eventually learn how to play a piano, do architecture, design dresses, compute high-level physics, strategically organize highly complex business logistics, run a company, form abstract concepts like "individual rights", fly a plane, give speeches and much much more.

That once-helpless infant will learn one or more languages, by herself, by the age of three. She can learn the basics of human survival (simple math, reading, writing) by the age of 6, like some kids do, or casually learn it all by the age of 10 – BY HERSELF.

She will understand the simple human concept of "next week", which no other animal on Earth does. She understands TIME. Lower animals don't know "time". They don't need it. They have no complex mental structure that allows for planning.

Her vocabulary at the age of two will be a minimum of 200 words, by the age of three 1,000 words, by the age of six 10,000 words, and by adulthood 30,000+ words.
Learning words and rules and principles will be almost an effortless exercise for Claire's brain. If the lower animals could understand the difference between themselves and Claire, well, they might call her a "god". They might say, "How does she DO all that?!"

And YET …

And yet there is something inside Claire's head that is even MORE alien to the lower animals.

Free will. Claire can think and make complex choices.

Scientists call it "volition" – the ability to actually conceptually choose between this thing and that thing at any given moment, the ability to NOT do something, or go on a hunger strike, or save money, or take gymnastics instead of ballet, or be honest or dishonest – the ability to pick between long-term and short-term options and run her life into the ground or towards ultimate happiness.

She's got the ability not only to understand anything in the universe, but to choose between a million different options in a lightning stroke of determination or after several months of close inspection of alternatives, including a career.

In fact, the ONLY way Claire or any human can survive and flourish is to make good choices all the time or nearly all the time. The lower animals do not have or NEED volition. They are built to act on instinct to survive. We don't have those instincts. We have to plan things and conceptually understand the world to make our decisions.

But … But our volition must be free from outside authority to pick and choose what things to do to achieve the great things in our lives that we choose to pursue, to give our lives meaning, to turn our lives into symphonies. We must be free from other people's demands upon us in our pursuits.

The only way that young Claire can be happy is if her volition, her free will, is not interfered with by us Care-Friends and others. She must choose her own paths.

Let's Leave Her Alone

And YET …

And yet, for thousands of years, most parents have assumed that Claire's mind isn't so special or that it isn't very motivated or that it has something evil or destructive inside it or that it must be controlled from Day One.

Plato himself believed (in his Republic) that infants should be taken immediately from the arms of their mother and raised anonymously by elitist outsiders, and he believed that only a select few humans were born to have integrity and intelligence – and to run everyone else's lives. Ha!

Unfortunately, this has been the mistaken belief of societies for hundreds of generations. In a way, many parents have the same belief concerning the running of their children's lives.

For thousands of years, parents have been riding the young Claires and Charlies of the world like they were ignorant and stubborn – forcing them into learning camps (schools) as if Claire and Charlie couldn't learn things and choose things by themselves, forcing them to be obedient as if that were actually conducive to independence and happiness in life, forcing them to NOT do this and to DO that, as if they couldn't understand things if those things were explained well and thoughtfully to them via direct and "grown-up" communication always. (After a child turns about two, "cute" talk is condescending and tells them that they are inferior.)

Even the very best of parents around the world take Claire's mind for granted and insist on some kind of control of daily habits or learning or obedience, instead of being the Happy Oak Tree who lets her live and let live and explains in a firm but pleasant way what the only rule is: "Have fun, sweetie, but be sure to not interfere with anyone else's fun exploration and enjoyment of life."

The best of parents will even let babysitters and day-care centers and "early-education" centers take control of their children for hours each day – as if EVERY SINGLE MOMENT of Claire's life is not absolutely vital for her free will in running her own life and not being interfered with. Her volition, her free will, is crucial for her complete confidence that she is running her life.

All children have the RIGHT to run their life every single moment. They MUST have it, or else their lives begin to not have their own meaning and self-fullness.

The control attitude towards children is what has to change if we are all to have happiness and freedom and a nonviolent society. We have to honor their mind and their free will, so they can make their own mistakes, feel the full authority of their minds to execute their values every second, and never feel the need to rebel against others trying to control them.

We are around our Claires and Charlies an enormous amount of time, but we must leave Claire and Charlie ALONE in their endeavors when we are not joining them (with their permission).

Only then will they become self-made men and women – happy, self-directed, productive, benevolent men and women in complete charge of their lives with no worries about others' opinions about what they do with their life.

We must set the Brain Child free to make of her life as she wishes.

Chapter Seven

Children Have Rights
The Birthright of the Rational Animal

In a few chapters, I begin getting into the fun nitty-gritty of raising our kids to be free, but I haven't yet given proof that we have rights – adults AND kids – or explained WHY we need to prove it, to be fully free.

In fact, nobody had given such proof until 60 years ago. That is surprising to me, but it is true. Until the 1950s, no great thinker for thousands of years ever actually proved why we have the right to be free. Incredible!

Each of you believes that you have rights in modern society. You believe that you have a right to your life, your property, your money, your liberty, and your pursuit of happiness. You have a right to NOT be interfered with by other people or by the government while you are pursuing your happiness. We don't have total freedom, unfortunately, but we believe we should.

But what if some people in America or another nation say, "Well, we believe that you DON'T have those rights!" An Englishman named Thomas Hobbes said this about 350 years ago, and he was certainly not alone in saying so. There are many voices around the world saying this now. And even in America, we are told what to do all the time by the government, and our money is taken from our paychecks at work, without us even seeing it, among other liberty losses.

So if we are saying we have rights and others are saying we really don't, what do we do, to ensure that we don't lose our rights completely?

Proof.

We have to PROVE we have rights and WHY we have rights, so that anyone telling us we don't have rights won't have a leg to stand on. That way, we can get up every morning knowing, by damn, that nobody has a right to mess with us or our kids. We know it in our brains because we know the proof behind it – just like we can prove we are honest if somebody calls us a liar. Our proof is in our argument, in the facts.

As it is in America now, a neighbor can call the government because the neighbor sees your kids outside playing on a school day. Government officials can come to your home and demand entrance allegedly out of "concern" for YOUR kids. Your kids allegedly don't have the right to play during school hours in many parts of America.

This is just one of thousands of examples of how rights are violated in America and around the world every day. The government says you must buy health insurance or you will be fined. You are told you must get a driver's license to drive your own car. You are told you must vaccinate your children. You are told you must register with the government to own a gun. You are told you must pay high taxes. You are told you can't text on your phone even while stopped at a traffic light. You are told you can't give large amounts of money to your kids or you'll be taxed heavily for that, even though it's YOUR money you are giving away.

The list goes on endlessly. We don't have full rights in America, and it won't change until we all understand what rights are and where they come from – until we understand the PROOF for rights and insist on having our rights all the time, for ourselves. Frankly, a revolution for rights is needed.

I'm just talking about adults in the above paragraphs. Though adults have lost some of their rights in "1st World" countries, they have it better than kids do.

Hitting children ("corporal punishment") is banned entirely in 46 countries around the world, but it's still legal in 152 nations, including the United States, where hitting children at home is allowed in all 50 states. Hitting children at school has been banned in about half of the U.S., but it is still legal in the other half of the country.

HITTING kids!

In the Bible, Solomon said that parents only love their children if they strike them when the parents don't like what the kids are doing. This has been the paradigm throughout history. It is changing somewhat, and that is terrific, but severely violating children's rights is still standard in most of the world.

I would imagine (and sincerely hope) that the readers of this book don't hit their children, but having rights goes further than not being hit. Having rights primarily means being able to run your own life – AND not being hit while doing so. It means we and our kids get to do whatever we wish with our lives every single second – without being controlled and without being hit.

We are not violating rights by preventing our small kids from running into traffic, and we would do the same favor for a friend who got a little fuzzy-headed and started walking in front of traffic. You haven't coerced your child or your friend in that circumstance, and you haven't taken away their rights. You simply jumped in to prevent harm to someone you love. After they are safe, they are free to again pursue their happiness AWAY FROM TRAFFIC.

The idea of "rights" for humans is hundreds of years old, but it wasn't until the 1950s that someone actually came along (in America) and PROVED that humans have rights. Her name is Ayn Rand. She was revolutionary. So let's talk about that proof that we need – to justify our rights and our kids' rights.

America's Founders and Ayn Rand

The Founding Fathers of America came close to getting "rights" right. They were correct about the fact that rights exist, but they wrongly thought that they were "endowed by their creator" or the "natural" product of "nature's god". They didn't fully understand "rights" and therefore couldn't explain specifically what rights were and where they come from. So they, basically, just took a shot in the dark and said, "Well, they come from a creator, so there's no arguing about it. Enough said."

Because they said it that way, anyone could come along and say, "Well, no, MY creator says we don't have rights, and there's no arguing about it. Enough said." Muslims and Marxists and others say this now. Marx and Hegel and Hobbes and Bentham and others were more inventive and said, "Well, no, the rules of society mean that we don't have rights. Enough said." They just substituted "rules" for a "creator" and came to the same rights-violating conclusions.

Their misunderstanding unfortunately led to the enslavement or oppression of entire groups of people, including women, children and people of different colors and races. It's a giant failing that we are still reeling from today, as Americans lose more of their freedoms with each passing presidential administration and Congressional term.

Our Founders had studied the idea of rights by John Locke and others, but Locke didn't fully understand rights either. He also linked them to a "god".

The Founders, who proved quite well why The Colonies should break from Britain, should've realized that they would have to prove "rights". Instead, they put themselves into a conundrum, making it to where they would have to prove that there WAS a creator, and then they would have to prove that that creator "endowed", and then they would have to prove exactly what was endowed – and then they would have to prove why the heck they even had to bring a "creator" into the rights discussion anyway.

What a mess!

The good news is that Ayn Rand cleared up this mess about 60 years ago, making it quite clear why all humans have rights in society – so that all races, both sexes, all ages of people are free from birth. It is my hope that her ideas will lead eventually to the liberty of billions around the world, including children.

Rand discovered that rights come from the fact that humans have rational minds that can only survive and be happy if the mind and its free-will are not interfered with by outsiders – like other people or government. It must be free from the instigation of force by an outsider while we are on our path to happiness, using our free will to make choices that are directly linked to the goals we are pursuing.

She recognized that only the individual human can know what makes him or her happy, and they must be free from coercion (outside force) to act on the conclusions of their minds – all the time, for their own happiness, their own self-fullness.

She identified and explained how the mind works with the facts of reality to integrate those facts into concepts (words) while in pursuit of goals (values), and that any interference with that pursuit and integration leads to the loss of happiness and fulfillment.

She realized that all animals seek survival and contentment, but that the lower animals do this instinctually. Humans do it "conceptually", which is much more complex and sophisticated, necessitating complete freedom for survival and happiness. Nobody, she said, has the right to force us to do anything we don't want to do. If they do use force, it undermines our conceptual process and happiness.

Each of us is unique, she said, and only EACH of us can know what will make us happy, using our brain to achieve that happiness within liberty.

It doesn't just apply when we are 18 years old and "magically" become adults. It applies from the moment we are born. Though we can't make any conceptual choices or goals in the first year of our lives, that inability does not eradicate our rights any more than Claire in a coma, unable to make conceptual goals or choices for a while. All humans have rights.

Here's what Ayn Rand said about rights 50 years ago:

"A 'right' is a moral principle defining and sanctioning (someone's) freedom of action in a social context. There is only one fundamental right (all the others are its consequences or corollaries): a ... right to (one's) own life. Life is a process of self-sustaining and self-generated action; the right to life means the right to engage in self-sustaining and self-generated action – which means: the freedom to take all the actions required by the nature of a rational being for the support, the furtherance, the fulfillment and the enjoyment of (one's) own life. Such is the meaning of the right to life, liberty and the pursuit of happiness."

Ms. Rand added the following:

"The concept of a 'right' pertains only to action – specifically, to freedom of action. It means freedom from physical compulsion, coercion or interference by other(s)."

So it is our job as parents to ensure our children's freedom of action, and ensure that they don't attempt to compel, coerce or interfere with us or others.

It isn't our job to prepare our children for life. They'll conduct their own symphony. It is only our job to ensure their rights are protected while they conduct themselves as they go through life on their own path – as they take their ACTIONS.

Because we love them, we will join them in activities and ensure they are safe without helicoptering them. We will provide explanations and definitions, share our own curiosity of life in thousands of situations with them, share our judgment with them when they are interested, give our own honest opinion always, and be the Happy Oak Tree that is just as firm a moral guide to them as the oak tree in the yard is a solid object they must acknowledge.

We will be self-full while helping and protecting our children, and they will be self-full in their free exploration of their fulfilling lives.

Pets Are Cute, But ...

To put more accent on what rights are and how amazing our children are, let's talk about how different they are from our pets and other animals – and why those animals do NOT have rights.

We humans are so highly functional and conceptual that we TALK to ourselves. Lower animals DON'T talk to themselves. They can't. Talking is a conceptual ability using highly conceptual tools (words) to represent THINGS in reality and to organize those things in abstract form, so that we can effectively run our lives and run our worlds and make complex decisions.

It is a very high brain function that only Claire and the rest of us have. Lower animals don't know they will die one day. They can't CONCEIVE it. We can and do. We understand "time" and dimension, past and future, death and life, good and bad, high and low, winning and losing. Lower animals don't even realize they are alive. They just DO things. They have no "me". They cannot put life into a context of "length of time". They know no lengths of anything. They don't need to know it. They act on instinct. They're built that way.

When we have pets – even when so-called "animal rights activists" have pets – we treat them differently than we do children or other adults. We give our pets the food and drinks and toys that WE want to give them. We don't (can't) ask them what they want. We make them live in cages, rooms, houses and yards at our whim. We pet them and hug them when WE want. We trim their nails when WE wish. We never ask for their permission. We "put them to sleep" when we decide it's what WE want to do. We love them, you bet, but we control them – because they don't have rights.

We butcher lower animals for our food and survival. Lower animals kill each other for the same reason, without the least thought of impropriety – without the least thought of murder or wrongdoing. Without the least THOUGHT. Even the highest lower animals do this: dolphins, monkeys, dogs, elephants, etc. That's what they DO. They cannot stop to think conceptually: "Let's see, is this right or wrong?"

There is no right or wrong for animals. There is just the momentary experience of the life in front of them. They do not have a free will or conceptual mind that must be protected from coercion from outsiders.

They are cute and have rudimentary emotions, but they cannot THINK. We can. We can testify in court, we DO understand right and wrong. We can DO right and wrong. And there is NO right and wrong in relation to others in a society if there are no rights. If you have no rights, then anyone can do anything to you that they wish. You can do no wrong to other humans if they don't have the right to be left alone. But they do – both adults and children – because of that wondrous 3-pound brain that Claire and the rest of us have.

Our brain's existence and conceptual ability give us rights!

This doesn't mean that we should go around abusing pets. Any such person has a screw loose, frankly. But it does mean that we do with pets as we please – unlike Claire and other humans, whom we are not allowed to interfere with.

And YOU Have Rights Too

I've talked so much about the little Claires and Charlies of the world having rights, so maybe you're feeling a little left out as a parent.

Of course you have rights. You've had them since you were an infant, but they weren't honored (by your parents, by the government, or by others).

As caretaker and Care-Friend, you keep your rights as you are raising your child. You will navigate those rights with each other the same way you navigate rights with friends who have come to your house or with coworkers or with neighbors. There are proper rules of property ownership and personal space that must be navigated by all parties, and we'll talk a lot about that concerning children and YOU in the following chapters, giving examples of how to handle many of the situations.

The Birth Right

I'm going to drive home this "children's rights" point just a bit more before we move on (after all, it IS the title of this book!).

Humans get rights the moment they are born BECAUSE they are the conceptual animal. They never have to prove they are human. They obviously are. There are no age requirements for rights, just like there are no size requirements or height requirements or racial requirements or hair-color requirements or test requirements or gender requirements. All humans have rights.

A human being, upon separate existence from her birth mother, automatically HAS those rights in perpetuity, as long as she doesn't severely violate someone else's rights later in life and is sent to jail or prison. Claire doesn't get her rights at the age of three or eight or 13 or 16 or 18 or 21 or 24. She gets them the moment she breathes her first breath of fresh air!

It's exciting to think of really. It puts a big responsibility on our shoulders to ensure that we acknowledge her rights and protect them always.

But, coincidentally, it also takes a huge load OFF our shoulders that has been felt by all parents throughout history: We don't have to take the responsibility to ensure that they become great people and become what WE want them to be. It's THEIR responsibility, and it's one, frankly, that they enjoy having. They get to choose everything.

What I've seen with my free-born child and some others who are her friends is that they actually make great choices nearly all the time and are extraordinarily happy and content all the time because they are running things in their own lives.

It was their birth right, after all.

Chapter Eight

The Mighty Are NOT Fallen
Kids Are Born Clean As a Whistle

We've all see newborn infants like Claire. They are lovely, innocent, cuddly. You just want to pick them up and smooch them!

But!

But, could it be that inside Claire's new big head she's hatching evil plans to take over the universe and enslave billions?

Could it be that in that very moment you're looking at your newborn that he or she is thinking, "I'll have this gullible, grinning big human eating out of my hand within two years and will scorch the Earth with audible napalm till I get what I want?!"

Could it be that all infants are born "fallen", as we've been told for thousands of years – with a natural inclination to do bad, to disrupt others, to rebel, to blithely rampage across a house or grocery store, to shout obscenities at one and all?

No. Of course not.

Children (and adults) are not "fallen". They are born "clean", with nothing at all in their minds. But they are eventually MADE to fall – by bad parenting, by not honoring rights to life and self-determination.

In one of the great ironic misconceptions through the centuries, it was adults causing kids to be bad – and then the adults simply assumed that the kids were born that way, after making them bad.

Humans have free will, and they can choose to do bad or do good, choose to be productive and creative, or choose to be lazy and parasitical. They can choose to be an astronaut or a thief – or any of thousands of other good or bad things in life. But it is extraordinarily difficult to make good decisions if someone else is attempting to forcefully run our lives.

The End of Ignorance

Most adult humans say that when a child begins thinking pretty well and understanding the world that that is the "end of innocence." The adults don't mean that phrase in a good way. That say it with dread, "Oh, my baby isn't innocent anymore."

In a sense, the adults are right about the "end of innocence," because the child is beginning to UNDERSTAND. It is a quite exciting and novel time for the child and for adults who love knowledge and choice in the world. But the end of innocence really is the "end of ignorance". And that should be a GOOD thing! It is the "beginning of learning". Even as adults, we can remain innocent (honest and carefree and loving) if we know we are free and demand to be free and are in charge of our lives.

It doesn't mean that something evil is about to pop out of children like a Hydra with nine heads as they begin to work with the world and challenge the world. It is the beginning of The Incredible Journey. It is their beginning to acknowledge and to change the world to their liking, as we adults do.

Claire and other children are just as cute and innocent as they appear when taking their first breath. There is nothing hidden in their minds, like a virus, that will automatically LEAP OUT and insist that they do horrible things or be unruly or be unkind or unjust or lazy or unmotivated.

They simply have that Path of Least Resistance survival pursuit of things that you'll sometimes have to handle, but there is no "evil spirit" within, as religions and many academics have unfortunately insisted upon for centuries. Claire is a "blank slate", a clean and pristine tablet awaiting imprinting by her boundless pirate curiosity and integration. She'll travel from utter ignorance to sublime understanding.

Centuries of Nonsense

The belief that children are naturally bad is a historical problem called skepticism: the belief that the human mind is an inferior and incapable organ for handling the world. It is a belief that the mind is essentially rotten inside and can't make heads or tails of the outside world, and that the mind requires artificial rules (commandments, outside regulators, monitors) to keep it reined in.

Many parents don't realize that they've internalized this belief before even having children, so they go about raising their children with this in mind, leading to control and punishment because the children allegedly "need it" to not be "naturally bad".

This "skepticism" of children and their amazing minds truly needs to stop, if we are to set them free and all of us free. Except for Ayn Rand, all philosophers and writers of the last 3,000 years have had this skepticism of children and adults, so it would seem that now is the time to put an end to this harmful era of humankind.

The millennial misfortune can be broken by us. It all starts with the incredible birth.

Chapter Nine

The Path of Least Resistance
Getting What They Want – What They Really Really Want

I talked earlier about how all of us take the Path of Least Resistance to get what we want and need in our lives, but kids haven't learned yet how to always take the Path without getting in others' way.

Young kids aren't bad. They just don't have the knowledge or mental control yet to keep their Path out of others' Paths – or they have learned from weak adults that they CAN get in others' Paths to get what they want.

The minds of children are naturally inclined to do two survival things after infancy:

1) Acquire knowledge
2) Acquire things

And toddlers do it with the reckless abandon of a pirate. They continue to do it as they get older – and in fact all of us do it our entire lives, starting around age 1.

What young children haven't learned yet is what we adults already know: how to acquire knowledge and things without harming others' rights.

Children and adults seek to go down paths to acquire those two things – the shortest paths possible. The world is more fun if there is little resistance on our paths to getting what we want. We don't want to waste our most valuable commodity: Time.

For older children and adults, it's a car or a house or a perfume or clothes or the newest phone. Desiring the shortest path possible to get these things is one reason we like Google so much: It has made our search path much quicker. In fact, technology is often built with the idea in mind to save us time, to shorten our Path, because most of us want to get things done more quickly – to save time.

We take this path in virtually every aspect of our lives, whether it is putting clothes in certain places in the closet, or having an extra roll of toilet paper ready near the toilet, or getting a dishwashing fluid that doesn't leave spots, or not allowing colored drinks on the white couch, or not speeding in places where there are usually cops. All of these actions save us time and cut down on the resistance we have in life to achieve our goals.

Us moral adults have learned that we do all of the above and much more while ALSO not violating others' rights. We are conscious of others and their desire to go down Paths of Least Resistance as well. If we are at someone's house where they ask that nobody drink wine on the couch, we adults oblige them, of course. We might think they are a little persnickety, yes, but we do oblige them. Our Path of Least Resistance aligns with theirs: We both wish to have pleasant conversation in which neither party is upset, and we both wish to honor the others' rights.

THIS is what young children haven't learned yet because they haven't been around long enough to learn it. We can't hold that against them. They are acquirers and doers, just like us, but they haven't learned yet how to acquire without disturbing others. That's where our Oak Tree comes in.

Children aren't born bad. They are new people on a planet with a thousand playthings in front of them. Once we understand this, it becomes easier to deal with them as a Happy Oak Tree. "Oh, they just need to learn in this situation what the boundaries are." All they need is a little firm and loving guidance and explanation and boundaries.

It will take many situations, hundreds of them, before they fully get it, and they will even occasionally make a mistake up until about 12 or so – and even every once in a while after that, as all of us adults do in a forgetful moment. So we should never think that our Happy Oak Tree ever dies or withers. We have to have it always for our kids and for our friends and family – because "S**T Happens".

Morality (doing the right or wrong thing in the pursuit of goals) is a highly abstract and difficult thing for kids, even the brightest of kids, to fully understand and integrate. It's sometimes easier for them to keep doing a bad thing rather than to listen to us – unless we make it harder for their Path by being the steady Oak Tree who won't give up.

When they wish to acquire or do something that may harm them or violate the rights of us or others, then we understand that their Path will have to be altered. They will need to understand that you, the Care-Friend, have just stepped in to give RESISTANCE – interrupting their Path.

Now their Path of Least Resistance has become the path of MOST resistance – because YOU are the resistor. If you remain an Oak Tree in such situations, they will seek to avoid such a bad scenario with you so badly that they will change their desire and behavior and PATH like clockwork.

For example, let's say your 3-year-old is in the living room with you and suddenly wants a toy from his bedroom. Instead of going around the glass-top coffee table, he decides it would be much faster to simply climb on it, run across it, jump off it and dart to the bedroom. It happens so fast, there's nothing you could do to stop it. He hasn't done that before, so you didn't expect it.

Time to be the firm but loving Oak Tree. The two primary things to remember when you are being the Oak Tree are to always stay just on the facts and stay perfectly calm (though there's nothing wrong with showing a little anger at first, if you feel it, but be sure to get calm once your anger is mostly gone).

"Hey Charlie!"
(He turns around)
"That's my coffee table, darling, and it could break if you run across it or jump on it, Okay?"
"Oh, sorry, mommy."
"Will you be sure to go around it from now on please?"
"Yeah."
"K. Thanks. You going to get a toy?"
"Yeah." (He runs to the bedroom happy and never does it again)

All of the above is said by you in a calm voice with benevolent but firm eye contact, staying just on the facts (YOUR coffee table. It could break. If he jumps on it.). You see that there was no maliciousness from him. He was simply on his Path, so you're simply informing him of the right path and what your property is.

If you've been the Oak Tree since he was 1, then he gets it right away and will honor your request. He already knows that you are a Happy Oak Tree who can't be messed with – and he loves you for it and wouldn't even think of trying to upset you.

If you haven't been the Happy Oak Tree since he was one, then he may have been malicious in this situation or just completely disregarding your right to your property because you have rarely offered firm resistance to his bad Paths.

In the scenario of having an unruly child who challenges you a lot, you'll have to learn to be the Oak Tree and remain the Oak Tree for longer periods during such confrontations, in order to change his disregarding behavior toward you and others.

You may have to physically hold him as he attempts to cross the table and talk with him firmly but benevolently while you're doing that, and let him know that you won't let go until he has promised to not cross the table. And after he has promised, you remain on high alert nearby to ensure that he indeed won't cross the table.

While you're handling the unruly child in this manner, you must always remain calm as rain, and yet perfectly firm – or he won't take you seriously. If he continually crosses the table and doesn't listen to you, then you may have to hold him for many minutes or even an hour at first, and you may have to do it several times, because he simply doesn't believe you'll be strong and he will test you. He'll get your Oak Tree soon enough, and your coffee table will remain untrampled for rest of his life.

Lightning Moments

I call these times the **Lightning Moments**. They happen instantly. Whether we are an Oak Tree or NOT an Oak Tree in that moment will determine the outcome of our child's life. They will learn boundaries for their happy journey now or, perhaps, never learn them and remain anxious for the rest of their days – visiting their bad Paths not just on you, but also on everyone around them.

No matter how surprised you are by these Lightning Moments, you must respond as quickly as lightning yourself (children always gauge your response time to see how confident you are) AND remain calm and firm. The great thing about remaining calm is that they see that you are in complete control of the situation and of YOU. This gives them comfort, and let's them know you're not being defensive and most likely being fair – you're simply doing what you know to be right and you won't have it any other way.

I'll be talking a lot more in a later chapter (Leverage II) about how to handle children on the wrong Path, who haven't been brought up with complete respect for their rights and who hold grudges and who get angry and lash out.

There are three very big things to remember during Lightning Moments:

1) Talk to them in the same voice you talk to your close adult friends: respectfully and firmly. Don't talk down to them, and don't lose your patience, because this is a big moment for them and for you.

2) Never take their property away from them or threaten to take their property away from them – except in brief moments when they are using their property to violate your rights, but then it is temporary, which you would do with a friend who was using their property to violate your rights. They must know that their property is always theirs, just like ours is ours. If we took their property away from them, we would be telling them they don't actually own it, and that any toy or car or phone or clothes they ever get from us is not actually theirs. They have eminent domain on their stuff. Not us. If you want to lose your children's trust, try taking their property. (Please don't.) I'll talk more later about how we use Leverage, especially with older kids, such as acknowledging that their phone is theirs but that WE pay for their phone service and Wi-Fi and those could be shut off.

3) Never EVER punish. We cannot punish other humans in our lives, because we do not own them. We can tell them that we will not be around them anymore, but that isn't punishment towards them. It's simply us being self-full and letting it be known that we can't be self-full around that person anymore, so we are removing ourselves from their circle. In the above "coffee table" scenario, it is up to us Care-Friends to ensure that it plays out the way we Oak Trees will insist it plays out. If it doesn't play out the proper way, it is OUR fault. And when things are OUR fault, we shouldn't go around punishing others, including children.

If you stay calm and fair and firm ALWAYS as that Happy Oak Tree, children will learn a NEW path of least resistance AWAY from a previous bad path (the coffee table) because they know you will resist and make it difficult for them. Eventually, they will stay away from the coffee-table path because they respect you highly and therefore respect your property.

After a while, once 3-year-old Charlie gets to be about 4 or 5 (at the latest), he learns that this new path is actually the good path anyway because he is honoring others and wishes to be honored himself. He feels good about his actions.

The Path Is A Good Thing

As I said at the beginning of this chapter, the Path of Least Resistance is a good thing for all of us if we don't harm others. It's a survival thing. It's a happiness thing. It's a time-saving thing. It's NOT a bad thing. Children SHOULD want to get things and do things in their lives as fast as they can, just as we adults do. The ONLY thing they have to learn (from YOU) is that they simply can't run over you and others while they're doing it – and they cannot EXPECT us to do for them what we simply don't want to do.

Once we understand this Path of Least Resistance survival mode, it actually puts a lot of things they do in proper perspective and can help us keep a cool head when "situations" arise. Heck, it can be pretty darn funny sometimes.

"Hey, Alex, um, you smell like poop. Did you wipe after going to the bathroom?"
"No."
(curious smirk) "OK, soooooo … mind telling me why didn't you wipe?"
"I dunno. I wanted to play my game. I didn't have time." (path of least resistance)
"Oh, I see. Of course. … Well, I guess you know that now you'll be smelling that poop while you're playing, huh?" (facts)
"Yeah."
"And I guess you know that it's gonna start itching pretty bad in about an hour, huh?" (facts)
"Yeah."
"And I guess you know that you're gonna get sores down there in about two hours, huh?" (facts)
"No." (getting his attention)
"And I guess you know that aliens from space will come live on your sores and build green blobs of goo on your bottom in four hours, right?" (kids love humor)
(laughing) "Noooooooooooo they won't!"
(chuckling) "OK, yeah, the alien-goo thing ain't happening. But, hey, look, it's kinda nasty having that poop on your rear, and I don't really want to be smelling it either, so what do you say we do a quick cleanup in the bathroom and put your game on pause? I'll help you, so we'll be done in, like, a minute."
"OK." (gets up and darts to bathroom slapping back of pants, shouting, "You better not come, aliens!")

(If a child like Alex hasn't really chosen a bad Path yet, then humor grabs their attention, and puts them in a good mood to think about what's happening.)

Children raised around Oak Trees will go to the bathroom with you. A lot of children not raised around Oak Trees wouldn't. You'll need to ask them to go somewhere else to play to honor your space. You'll need to become The Resistor on their path. You can't force them to clean themselves or do it yourself without their permission, because THEY own their bodies and the right to their bodies. But you CAN let them see what happens when they choose the bad path. They learn!

"No, I don't want to go to the bathroom."
"Alrighty, well, I'm not wanting to smell the poop, so you'll need to go find someplace else to play so I don't have to smell it. It smells horrible (facts). If you change your mind and need my help just let me know. Thanks, Alex."

In a pretty good relationship between parent and child, that would be the end of it, and he'd probably come back for your help in a bit – when he starts ITCHING! (the good part of letting him experience his own consequences on the poop instead of forcing him to clean himself is that he learns first-hand the facts of life and makes his own choices and is in charge of himself – and of course that you were honoring his right to himself.)

In a relationship that has been rough around the edges, he may tell you he's not going to another place to play – in effect, telling you he doesn't care about your smelling his poop and that you just have to live with it. An adult friend obviously wouldn't do such a thing, but in this case, you'll have no choice but to let Alex know that your happiness won't be compromised by this bad Path.

Time to be the Oak Tree!

"I'm not going to go!"
(in a matter-of-fact voice addressing him as you would an adult) "I'm not gonna smell your poop, Alex. If you want to, that's your choice, but I want clean air, so if you don't go, I'm gonna have to move you to another place. Do you want to move, or am I going to be moving you? Your choice, big guy."

At this point, virtually all children will go (not happily, but they GET that you're being an Oak Tree).

For those who don't go even then, it's the showdown, the Lightning Moment. You pick them up and quietly move them to their room as many times as necessary, even if they keep coming back and even if it lasts for several minutes or even a couple of hours – until they realize one of the most important points of your relationship: that you will NEVER give in to what is wrong. You will ALWAYS calmly be an Oak Tree, no matter how long it takes and no matter how difficult the situation is, to get done what has to be done – and you'll do it with complete serenity and confidence, knowing that your actions now will set the future tone of your relationship and your child's relationship to the rest of the world.

Bad children can be turned around in a matter of a few months with these kinds of consistent Oak Tree actions. I've seen it happen with a few of my daughter's friends.

I'll revisit many more examples of children of all ages (including teens) in later chapters about using Leverage and handling the Path of Least Resistance and being a Happy Oak Tree. (Yes, I know, if say "Happy Oak Tree" one more time …!)

But remember that the resistance is YOU. You are The Resistor. You are the boundary of bad Paths. If you offer no resistance to the child when he wants to do something bad, he will continue to do it. If you offer little resistance, he will manipulate you and continue to do it. If you offer a lot of resistance but eventually cave, he will continue to do it after wearing you down. If you offer total resistance, he will stop doing it – maybe not immediately, but soon.

The problem with many female parents is that they have "too much empathy" for their children. They don't want to see them struggle with something or feel bad or get mad. But if you really love your child, you have to look past these feelings and be the Happy Oak Tree in the Lightning Moments – for their sake and for YOUR sake. Life is hard, and people out in the world are hard, so what better place for your children to learn about the hard facts of reality and the good Path and rights than with the most caring person they know: YOU?

The problem with most male parents is that they are the opposite side of the spectrum from the female parents. The males often "don't have enough empathy" about what the child is feeling in the moment or about the child's struggles. The male parents often just want the Path fixed NOW. So male parents often take a commanding and distant tone. But, again, if you truly want growth and independence in your children in a tough world, you will simply be the calm, patient, caring Oak Tree.

Mothers tend to bend and to be worse than fathers on the firmness, but fathers tend to go in the equally bad direction of being overly firm or stern or authoritarian, instead of both being calmly firm and loving.

The product of either tendency by the parents is the same: children who never quite gain full self-esteem and self-fulfillment – they are never fully self-full and happy. Now is the time to help them be happy kids that turn into happy adults.

You don't want to stop their Path of Least Resistance discovery. It's a good thing. You only want to ensure that the Path is not over you and others.

If you offer ultimate, non-bending resistance, the child will stop doing it and will find something nicer and better to do. It works this way every single time, and you may have to prove more than once that you NEVER give up – and you may have to spend a fair amount of time at first showing that you never give up until they BELIEVE you.

The degree to which you resist bad actions usually sets your child's outlook forever. I've seen very few people, unfortunately, change from the way they were as children. You set their psychology towards others NOW. If you start early with the confident resistance, they BELIEVE you and will seldom challenge you on it. If you don't start early, they won't believe you, but you can still convince them and get them on the Path of honoring rights.

Kids (and adults) don't like Oak Tree resistance to bad Paths. Frankly, they want the resistor to cave in the moment. But adults and kids DO want good relationships. So, at some point in your Oak Tree resistance, they cave and realize you are right.

Afterward, there is no stress in the relationship, and it is lovingly deeper, calmer, more trusting and more bonding.

My own daughter would often climb into my arms for love soon after I had to be The Resistor. They get a sense that they are doing bad. They want your confidence and direction. They may not like it in the moment, but they feel themselves calm down in a few moments with the comforting feeling that you were there for them and were as beautifully firm as the oak tree.

Calm, firm resistance to a bad Path of Least Resistance creates a loving, respectful, giving, confident child who is simply a joy to be around.

Pure Love Is Not Unconditional

When we pick our friends and spouses, we have conditions for them, and they have conditions for us. Those conditions are honesty, fairness, good communication, affection, hard work, and the honoring of each other's right to self-direction and determination.

Those are conditions!

And there are LEVELS to love. Those levels are based on the conditions we have. We have more conditions for a spouse (love, honesty, honor, respect, mutual interests) than we do a casual friend. We have more conditions for our child (honesty, respect, integrity, commitment) than we do for family members.

Many people when they get married or have children decide to love them "unconditionally" – not matter what they do.

But what if a spouse yells at you fairly often and doesn't treat you with respect all the time? The love for the spouse is still there, but it's not as pure and sweet as it was before. He or she has broken one of the conditions for love: respect. That's why pure love is conditional – not unconditional.

And what if a child is persistently disrespecting you, insulting you, taking your things without asking, and taking advantage of you, do you still love them as much as you did when they weren't doing those things when they were younger? No. You don't. There must be respect (a condition) in a relationship to have pure love.

Yes, we still may love our spouse and child in the scenarios above, but that love isn't pure anymore because love DOES have its conditions – even with our kids.

In extreme cases of disrespect or even verbal abuse with a spouse, the earlier pure love may even turn into no love at all – because the spouse has severely violated your conditions for love. Such relationships may end at that point. The same may hold true for a teenager who has gotten equally disrespectful.

This is book is about attaining and keeping pure love – by honoring and respecting the rights and conditions of those around us.

Love actually means nothing if it is unconditional. If there aren't any conditions to love, why not love everybody? It would mean that you would love anybody and everybody, no matter what they did. But we must have good actions and good expression from someone to truly love them.

The same goes for our kids. We must have good actions and good expression from them. And the best way to ensure that is to be a very loving part of their lives and to be the Oak Tree when they go down the wrong Path. Otherwise, they will eventually stay on the bad Path and break some of those conditions I mentioned, making it very difficult to love them fully.

We can't love somebody "not matter what they do".

Children who sense an attitude of "unconditional love" are actually sensing weakness on the parent's part. They sense that the parent will put aside all conditions to ensure love. All children in this environment will simply run right over the parent and the parent's rights. The parent is usually flabbergasted that the child continues to run over her, not understanding why their unconditional love doesn't work. It never does. You HAVE to mix the Oak Tree with the love (and now I'm mixing metaphors!).

I don't know who came up with the phrase "unconditional love", but I sure wish they hadn't. It has been used as an excuse by many parents to let their children do pretty much anything. Truly unfortunate.

The fact is that we cannot "love them enough" to get kids to be good. Doesn't work with adults either. Humans don't work that way. Until a child becomes disciplined in their approach to their Path of Least Resistance and life, that child will be looking for weakness in others, in order to shorten their Path. The only thing that will be unconditional then is their understanding of where the weaknesses lie.

It isn't a cake-walk being The Resistor when our children (or anyone else) are violating our rights. It isn't easy to see the initial pain or confusion on their faces when we put our foot down. But if we truly care about them in those moments, we remind ourselves that it is absolutely necessary to be the Oak Tree – for their survival and happiness, and for OUR happiness. We sometimes have to remind ourselves that our conditions are real and they are necessary.

I'm not saying that our conditions for love mean that we walk around with our "judging hats" on all the time – though, in a sense, we are judging other people's actions all the time on our conditions of fairness, honesty, etc. So, I guess I AM saying we have our judgment hats on all the time, but we are trying to be just about it.

We all agree that life should be about the pursuit of happiness, and happiness depends on conditions. When those conditions are met, we are ecstatic and might even be jumping around with joy – so much so that people may think we're a little bit crazy. (Ha!) So we are having fun, and time with our children should be the same: FUN. All relationships should be this way. And so this "fun" is the reason us Care-Friends have to have our conditions and be Oak Trees – so nobody is harming anybody on their Path of Least Resistance, so we can all have TONS OF FUN!

Pure fun and pure love require honesty, integrity, independence, justice and more. Children cannot respect and love a lying parent. That would be unconditional love. Parents cannot respect and love a lying child. That also would be unconditional. Simply being a part of a family doesn't give us a get-out-of-jail-free card on love. We can't just say "I'm family" and expect family members to love us. (That idea has run rampant through modern cultures, turning family reunions into Peyton Places.)

The only exception I would place on the above about unconditional love is the first year or so of our children's lives, before their brains start kicking in. In that first year or 18 months, we can't put any conditions on them or our love. They can't choose bad Paths during that time, so we just love and take care of them fully.

But starting around 18 months, our kids start understanding that they are taking either good or bad Paths around us. Once they get to about four or five years old, they definitely know they are taking either good or bad Paths, so we can expect a lot more from them. We can expect them to UNDERSTAND fully that they should start staying on their good Path, honoring themselves, honoring our rights, living a self-full life.

Chapter Ten

Leverage (One)
Use the Things You Own to Get Your Rights Respected

I've mentioned "Leverage" many times, but I haven't really expanded on this very important tool that us Care-Friends have – that ALL people have – to keep relationships respectful, to attain justice, and to alter bad behavior with every single person we come into contact with.

As long as we have something someone else wants or needs, we have Leverage to use (carefully) to ensure they treat us with respect. We can use that Leverage wisely to alter bad behavior or poorly out of spite, anger or manipulation. Obviously, I recommend the first use as a firm but benevolent way of correcting bad Paths.

All parents throughout history have had all the "power" in their relationship with their children up to a least age 12 and mostly to age 16 or 18 or beyond. This "power" can be used fairly and firmly – or it can be used to rule over children and make them "obedient".

One of the purposes of this book is to NOT raise obedient children. It is to raise FREE children who are independent and driven to succeed in life on their own, with complete creativity and a full understanding of their rights and the rights of others.

When I say "power", I mean LEVERAGE – the five things every human has and every child needs from the parent to pursue their happiness:

1) **Money** (to buy them what they want or need)
2) **Things** (food, TV, furniture, WI-FI, phones, cars, clothes, toys)
3) **Caretaking** (taking care of their needs)
4) **Communication/Interaction** (talking about and experiencing life)
5) **Love** (the affection they thrive on, and we thrive on)

These five things – money, things, caretaking, communication and love – can be TEMPORARILY removed from the child by the calm, rational, caring parent as the parent is being the Happy Oak Tree of guidance in ensuring that rights are honored in the household – not as a bludgeon and not angrily.

These are not our children's wants. They are our children's NEEDS. They have to have one or more of the above virtually every day of their lives until they are 16. They have to come to YOU to get those things. If they don't treat you or others right, you can then remove one or more of the Leverages above to correct a bad Path. After all, it is YOU who owns them, and people, including children, don't get them with just any kind of behavior. There are CONDITIONS – They have to EARN your Leverages from you.

In the first 18 months of our children's lives, before their brain kicks in pretty well, they get these Leverages for free, basically. But after that, they have to begin earning them by respecting our rights as much as we respect theirs.

For instance, let's say your 10-year-old boy is supposed to do the dishes, but he walks up to you and says he has done most of the dishes but won't do the pancake griddle because it's too "hard" to clean, which it obviously isn't, and you know it. You know that he is simply trying to pawn off the "hard" cleaning onto you or someone else. When you become the Happy Oak Tree and point this out with the facts and he still won't clean the griddle, then you can use your Leverage.

In a calm and content voice, you might say something like, "OK, Bradley, I get it. You don't want to do your job. I suppose you can go ahead and find somebody else to take you to your football practice, because it ain't going to be me, darling. I'm beginning to think that it might be too 'hard' to do that. I think I might read a book or something instead. Thanks for giving me some free time later."

After you say that, walk away calmly, because the situation is done for you. Do not attempt any more conversation on the griddle. Just contently say you're not interested. This calm but firm use of Leverage brings most children around within a little bit. I will talk in the Chapter on "Leverage (II)" about how to use even greater Leverage with those children who don't come around at this point.

Notice also how effective it is to use their same language against them. In this case you used the word "hard" to accentuate their deception in the moment, and they get to see the irony, and you get to have a little fun with it. You are the Happy Oak Tree, so you should be having FUN, even in tense moments. Those moments will pass successfully, if you hold your ground self-fully and stay on the facts.

As Oak Trees, we will use one or more of those Leverages occasionally to ensure that our free children understand that there are responsibilities that come along with freedom that are unbreakable, that our love is NOT unconditional – the same way we hold our friends' and family's feet to the fire. We love life and we are self-full, but we can only be that way if nobody walks over us, including our dear children.

Because we love our children dearly, it is never truly easy to do this. We don't like to cause them emotional pain or hardship with our Leverage – but it is that emotional pain and hardship that helps refine them and makes them responsible and WAKES THEM UP. We have to keep this in mind every single time, so that we stay strong.

And we have to be very careful with our Leverage. VERY careful. We don't use it out of spite or anger. We have to watch ourselves on this. We must use it with the full knowledge that it is temporary, and it is used to get their attention, with the design of altering their bath Path of Least Resistance away from violating others' rights.

When I said above that even love is a Leverage, that may have thrown up a few red flags to many of you. But we temporarily do this with adults we know.

If a friend or family member treats us badly, we might ask them not to call us for a while, until they will acknowledge what they did and apologize. You've just temporarily taken away your affection, your love, from the relationship. It doesn't mean you don't love them anymore, probably, but it does mean that you've decided right now that they don't deserve your full self. You used your love Leverage to alter their behavior. You're not punishing them. You're just fed up and not feeling the love – so you won't give it for a while. That is a good thing. Love has conditions.

Once our children reach about age four and understand the rules pretty well, this same Leverage can be used with them regarding love, with firm but benevolent comments like, "I don't think I want to be around you right now, love. I'm still upset that you threw a rock at my car" or (for older kids) "I'm still upset that you and your friends trashed the house during the sleepover".

This is entirely fair, and it is how you are feeling, and you are right – and the child KNOWS it. If you are right and you are acting justly, no child on Earth will stay mad at you for long. They really do know fairness and thrive on it. They will come back to you within seconds or minutes or, in the case of older children, within hours or days.

Children understand being upset and they understand that your love is conditional upon them honoring your rights. When you show that you're upset by essentially putting yourself in "Time-Out" away from them, they really get this. It is visceral. They will apologize and want to be in your lap (young children) or want to talk with you (older children). Your love is a mighty Leverage, and you can be fair in using it.

When I had to withdraw immediate love and affection from my daughter (about a dozen times in her first 12 years), our communication and respect afterward was off-the-charts terrific, with no lingering anger or bitterness. Just openness.

If our friends or family members slight us or disrespect us, we will take away some of our affection and some of our communication until they treat us better. If a friend has been borrowing our car, but then the friend brings it back with an empty tank of gas, we will tell them in a nice way that they need to go fill it back up. If they do it again, we see that they are being disrespectful of us and our belongings, so we will not let them borrow it anymore, until we feel a sincere enough apology and a recompense. And we will probably tell them we don't' want to be around them right now, if they don't handle the situation well.

To remove our things and ourselves from someone else is not punishment of them – though they may feel it is punishment. It is us saying, basically, "Hey, you know, I'm not going to be involved in this, so I'm outta here." We use our Leverage to remove ourselves or things from that person and situation, often temporarily, and we go along our merry way to our enjoyable Time-Out.

Someone once said, "I'd rather be by myself and happy than to be around people who don't respect me." I agree. That is a healthy attitude of self-fullness.

Our acquaintances who wrong us and experience us using Leverage against them see this and realize we are not a person to be toyed with. They also see that we're calm, and that is impressive and reassuring to them – letting them know it's probably not permanent and that it can be fixed.

The same kind of fairness properly works in a parent/child relationship. It isn't unfair to our teen-ager to say, "Hey, you know, I don't think I want to spend any time with you right now, if you're going to continue talking that way. I'm outta here. Let me know if things change or if you want to nicely talk about this. I'll be glad to talk, if it's going to be good for both of us." (no threats, just facts)

In that scenario, you are simply removing yourself and your love in the moment, letting the other person know that you've got proper rules and too much respect for yourself/time to stay involved in a bad Path that violates rights or is disrespectful. You've used your Leverage. You've gone to your blissful Time-Out to be self-full.

We carry our Leverage with us throughout our lives. People usually want something from us, and often it is good stuff, like our personality or our humor or our companionship or something we own and want to share. Because we have something others want, that gives us Leverage (a value) we can enjoy sharing or we can remove if things go south in the relationship.

It is perfectly fine and right for us to pull out our Leverage to ensure that we are respected and that our rights aren't being violated – as long as we do it with aplomb, with confidence and firmness and directness, without being malicious about it.

It's obviously OK to be angry about something and even argue about something, but when it comes time to pull the Leverage plug, it's time for calm, cool and collected. Otherwise, it is defensive or offensive, and it carries no gravity.

For any of you thinking right now, "I could NEVER do those things. It would be too hurtful and I love my child too much," then please prepare yourself for a relationship of occasional or ongoing disrespect. If you don't use your Leverage to get your proper respect, you'll never get it, and your child will never understand the boundaries and obligations of their rights. You have to stay strong in Lightning Moments!

Use It or Lose It

Nobody loves the person who lets others walk on them. I personally adored and loved my mom dearly, but as the years went by and I saw that she let my dad and others run over her, I couldn't help but lose respect for her. It was very painful to watch, and it was even more painful to feel as a child and as an adult. I would try to get her to talk back and stand up for herself, but she just wouldn't do it.

In the first year of our children's lives, there is no need to use Leverage because their volition hasn't kicked in yet and they can't CHOOSE to do harmful things. It would be fruitless because they wouldn't understand – not to mention that it would be just downright mean.

And between the age of 1 and the end of age 3, we try to use it sparingly because we can usually just use communication and determination to get things across.

But after THAT!

We can begin using our five Leverages with children completely when they are about 4 years old and have the conceptual ability to understand right and wrong and who they are. They can now understand WHY we're using Leverage and WHAT we're doing – the consequences of their actions and our actions.

But let me backtrack just a bit.

Some of you may be thinking, "Oh, yeah, what about the TERRIBLE TWOS?"

There is no such thing as the terrible twos in a close relationship, in which the parent has been a loving Oak Tree. The age of two is when children get fully mobile and are in full discovery mode – Aaahr Matie! They don't want anyone or anything getting in their way – their Path.

It is at this age that us parents must begin being full Oak Trees and drawing those lines on bad Paths. We communicate all the time. We explain that parking lots are fun but also dangerous. We explain that drivers in cars are often not careful and they often can't see us, especially small kids, when they are backing out. So we explain why we have to stay close together.

If the child insists on darting in parking lots, even after this explanation, then we explain why we must hold hands. If the child refuses to hold hands, then we explain why they can't go with us to the store (which all children love at that age). We use our Leverage of transportation to ensure that they will follow rational rules in parking lots. They will eventually respond well, if you hold your Oak Tree ground.

If we don't use our Leverage in this moment, then we lose it, and they won't respect the danger of the situation or us. If you decide to force them to hold hands, they will be resentful and angry, and they will lash out at you, or worse, dart into the parking lot – either in the store or in the car or soon afterward and forever. (I've seen this happen at Kroger at least five dozen times.)

Put Yourself in Time-Out

Putting a child in Time-Out is punishment and wrong. It tells them that they don't have a right to their own body and time – and that you are in charge of their body and time. It tells them that you OWN them, when, in fact, you only own yourself.

Since you own yourself, YOU can take a Time-Out – in a good way.

You aren't punishing yourself. You're just taking a pleasurable time away from someone who is not respecting you and won't listen to you. It's a blissful Time-Out. You decided on it. You've decided you're not getting the respect or actions that are necessary, so you're out of here – to do something more pleasant, until they begin to understand what they did.

Your Time-Out doesn't have to be just your removal of yourself from a situation. It can be a Time-Out on your possessions and money as well.

You can use Time-Outs on all five of your Leverages: Put a Time-Out on taking them places when they want. Put a Time-Out on cooking their dinner (let them fix something for themselves) or buying them the things they want. Put a Time-Out on the cash you give them or the Wi-Fi they use or the car they borrow or the fitness club you pay for. Put a Time-Out on your communication with them.

As I said before, you still honor their property and never ever attempt to take it away from them, but the fact of home life is that they need a whole lot of your property and time and love and care-taking and cash. So you are putting a Time-Out on YOUR things.

Those are the things you can rightfully take away temporarily because they are YOURS. By taking away only your owned things, you not only enforce their right to their own things, but also make it clear that YOU have a right to your things. And you make it clear that there are boundaries of actions that are necessary for access to your things. You insist that your property must be honored too – or you'll put your things in Time-Out for as long as necessary.

Talk Straight, Not Down

We can't use Leverage well if we don't treat our children as equals, talking to them with equal respect for their minds and rights. If we don't treat them as equals, then when we use Leverage, it will come across as mean and punishing. You simply can't beat straight-talking. Children LOVE it. No preaching.

We talk to them like adults – whether they are 2 years old or 16 years old. Children like being addressed with the full respect with which adults get addressed. They thrive on it. They realize, implicitly at first, that you respect their minds enough to say things how they are – that you don't expect them to be simpletons.

And they soon realize that we talk straight to them because we also EXPECT them to act mature, adult-like, in their lives. They will meet this expectation. When I say "adult-like", I mean that they understand the rules and the necessity for abiding by good rules, just like adults.

We don't take peremptory tones with them or act like rulers. We just say it how it is.

Kids understand and feel condescension, and they get plenty of that by other adults in their lives (my daughter used to roll her eyes when adults talked to her "like a child"). So they love us more because we don't talk to them like that.

The "Arsenal"

While having some ice cream with my daughter and friends a few months ago, a pleasant-looking (and acting) mom nearby said to her five-year-old daughter: "If you don't carry your little brother's shoes RIGHT NOW for him, we won't ever come back to this place to get ice cream!"

My daughter and her friends and my friend and I were dumbstruck. The woman's daughter was devastated and picked up her brother's shoes mournfully.

This is such a horrible and mean use of the Leverage that I hardly know where to start. This mom unfortunately turned her Leverage into an "arsenal".

The young boy was the MOM's son, not the daughter's son, so it was the mom's obligation to carry the shoes, not the daughter's. The mom used her arsenal to turn her daughter into a momentary slave, to take advantage of her, to take her daughter's rights away from her.

Our Leverage should be used only to highlight the fact that we, the Care-Friends, are being treated unfairly or some other person is being treated unfairly by the child, and that that simply won't be acceptable, and we will have to withdraw something from the relationship until that point is clearly accepted by the child. We only use our Leverage after we've faithfully tried communication: talking, explaining, outlining of facts about the situation.

This is not being "insensitive" – it is being REAL. It is the way of free people: quid pro quo (something for something). Prosperous and healthy relationships are NEVER one-way streets. You scratch my back, and I'll lovingly scratch yours, darling.

Some might call using Leverage "putting your foot down". OK, but I like to think of it more as "putting your good foot forward and keeping it there until all is good".

We use our Leverage without having to raise our voice, or using force. We might be upset and emotional at something our child did, and it's certainly OK to express our strong emotions then. In fact, we should express those emotions, as we do with our friends, to show that we were upset by the action. But being emotional shouldn't leak over into emotionalism – using our emotions to get revenge or punish. Once we've gotten over the emotional anger, we should immediately calm down and talk sensibly and fairly and justly, using only facts.

Using our Leverage also helps the child do their own thinking on their own actions, helping to create an independent, joyful and creative person.

They will see what the cause was and what the effect was, if you stand by what you say and do. "Mommy doesn't want to help me reach things in the cabinet when I won't stop making a lot of noise. ... She's being real nice about it, but I can see that she's upset. I can see that she's right. I need to stop making so much noise. It bothers her. I like her and don't want her to be bothered. ... AND I need some FOOD!"

What "mommy" has done here is to help ensure that her child begins to understand cause and effect and that others in the world desire things too, and that the child must get what she wants within that context of OTHERS and their rights.

I'm not talking about retracting food and drinks, like you would a dog you're training. I'm talking about temporarily withdrawing your help from getting the food or drinks – as much as possible, depending on the child's age. More importantly, I'm talking about helping the child understand clearly that your services depend upon you getting the respect you deserve.

Children begin to understand from the age of 2 what right and wrong are. They KNOW when they are doing wrong against another person. But they haven't learned and integrated the mental discipline yet (graduating between the ages of 2 and 10) to fully enact the principles of conduct necessary for full respect while they're going down their pirate Paths.

As most of us know, young children will run roughshod over an entire army of Roman soldiers to get a Snickers bar, if the children thought that was the easiest Path to the candy! (Frankly, I might be tempted too!) They are WIRED to acquire and survive and thrive – to GET what they want the fastest way possible, and to blithely leave destruction and messes in their wake – so our Leverage is the ONLY means of ensuring that the "bad pirate" doesn't happen.

Chapter Eleven

The Watchman
Protector of the "Inner Tone"

So let's begin this exciting hands-on journey of raising free kids – of being self-full Oak Trees of our happy pirates traveling down their Paths of Least Resistance.

In this chapter, I'll talk about infancy. In Chapter 12, I'll talk about toddlers. And in Chapter 13, I'll talk about using Leverage with kids ages 3 through 16 – for parents who haven't had kids yet, for those who have kids, and for parents who haven't raised their kids entirely free to this point.

Our care-taking in the first year of our children's lives is hard work, but it is perhaps the simplest and most straightforward – and yet it may be the most important when it comes to setting the "tone" of the relationship and setting our children's "inner tone" for how they sense the world. One prominent, respected psychologist calls this "inner tone" the core valuation.

Infants will either come out of that first year feeling taken care of and feeling like the world is a safe place – or they will feel uneasy and anxious about both.

So, after we first meet our new baby, we should have just one Prime Directive for the following 12 months or so: Make them feel good and safe and comfortable about their little world EVERY MINUTE OF THE DAY.

The challenging question for us can be: "Can I be so attentive with my baby that he can go the entire 12 months without crying even once?"

That may sound like it's crazy, but it's almost achievable. It is a clich in our world that babies cry, but it shouldn't be. If we are around our babies almost all the time and stay very attentive to their needs and their moods, we can catch them BEFORE they cry.

THAT should be our goal – to ensure that their inner tone about life is serene, that their core evaluation is bright and happy.

Babies usually cry only when they need something badly or are hurting. If it's just needing something badly, they almost always have "tell" signs, like a gambler, that let you know the crying is about to begin. So our goal is to be so watchful that we'll see the "tells" immediately and respond so fast that our baby doesn't even make it to the crying stage.

We are The Watchman.

There's been a lot of research that promotes letting babies cry ("Ferberizing") and a lot of research against letting them cry, so I'm not even going to mention all of that outside research specifically. Let's just get to the point that is often missed in research papers and studies: A baby crying is in NEED of something. Their crying means something is wrong. They're not crying for the heck of it. They aren't smart enough yet to manipulate us parents, so if they are crying or getting close to crying, there is a REAL need. Older children have wants and needs. Babies only have needs.

They have rights at this age, too, as I've mentioned, and that right is to get what they absolutely need in the moment to assuage the problem they are having or about to have. It is our job as loving Watchmen to watch them almost constantly and be near them almost constantly to ensure that they never even get to the crying stage. It can be a tough job, but they are irresistibly squeezable and lovable, so that helps!

On an anecdotal note, I noticed with my infant daughter and other infants of "Watchmen" that they were the happiest and most-content babies. The infants of parents who allowed their children to cry seemed restless and not completely content even when they were on the nipple.

So why should we even take any chances by letting them cry during that first year? Why don't we just ensure that our babies are perfectly comfortable and taken care of immediately when they begin to get restless or they get hurt? I know that as an adult, I would be upset if I were crying and my friends just looked at each other and said, "Oh, don't worry, she'll cry herself to sleep, or she'll get over it in a while."

Um, bye-bye, friends!

We are talking about our infant being with us for the rest of our lives as he or she grows. We should not be taking chances recommended by an outside Ferberizer when we could be potentially harming their first feelings about the world.

If we are great Watchmen, then the only crying our baby will ever do is when he has some quick discomfort or he feels pain from a fall or something. And in those moments, we obviously cradle him in our arms and say sweet-somethings while we take care of him. Babies like contact almost all the time.

As the ever-present, benevolent Watchman for Claire and Charlie, we always have in our mind that we are ensuring that their "inner tone" is sonorous and sweet.

I think it is in this year that they feel safe and loved or don't feel safe and loved – absorbing those feelings and taking them through the rest of their life – good or bad. It will begin their first feelings about how the world seems: safe or dangerous.

The Care-Friend is either on duty and is mindful and loving and ever-present, or the Care-Friend is not. Claire and Charlie feel lovable or not. They are worthy of attention or not. They are worthy of affection or not. They can't put all of that into words, but they feel it, one way or the other.

If we are watching them all the time and listening attentively to them and their moods, we should be able to catch them BEFORE they start crying about 90% of the time, if not more. If we care about their lifelong comfort with us and the world, we will do so. We will be The Watchman of their happiness.

Unfortunately and sadly, we've all seen anxious babies. They've been neglected or ignored or abused – a little bit or a lot. They never seem calm. Their eyes dart around nervously. Some of their parents have "allowed" them to cry themselves to sleep, and some of have done much worse – wreaking havoc on the inner tone.

As loving parents, it isn't enough for us to just love our infants. We have to take it a step further to be full-fledged Watchmen to protect that all-valuable inner tone.

Going Tribal

Babies want to sleep with their parents for the first year or two, or at least very near their parents in the same room.

In almost all primitive tribes, the parents and their tribal friends actually conduct this first year with infants pretty much perfectly. They carry the babies everywhere. They sleep with them. They watch constantly. The mother's breast is inches away. They are hands-on with playing and interacting. They CARE! There have been plenty of documentaries showing these first-year-babies in tribes NEVER crying. The mom is so close all the time that she senses the baby's moods and responds immediately.

THIS is the ideal Care-Friend in modern society, whether mom or dad or outside caretaker. Our busy lives make it much more difficult, but we can get pretty close to this ideal by focusing on it intently and carrying it through – and planning on it ahead of time before conception or at least before birth. The time will have to be set aside for this kind of intense care in the first year.

My daughter, Kathryn, was a day sleeper for the first 13 months – not a night sleeper! Ouch! We took turns staying up with her most of the night and holding her for those many months, with lots of 24-hour days and catnaps. We tried playing with her for a long time late at night, with the hope that she would be tired enough to sleep through the night. But after one hour of sleeping, she'd wake up and be ready to GO. Even drinking large amounts of breast milk in a bottle or being breast fed didn't seem to make her tired. But it was what is was, and we knew she would eventually adapt to our timetable, which she did around 14 months.

The thing that gave us patience on those difficult nights was thinking long-term about her comfort and inner tone. Without that comfort, we knew, raising her afterward would be a throw of the dice on her feelings about us and her world.

Without that PERFECT comfort of being cared for, children get uneasy, and that uneasiness can extend into a lifetime. I see this much too often with the 1-year-olds of acquaintances. Half the battle has already been lost. Maybe that battle can be won back by honoring of their rights afterward, but it makes it more difficult.

We also did research on restless babies and found that tightly swaddling them could ease their restlessness. It worked like a charm. Kathryn became perfectly happy and giggly when swaddled. Perhaps this is some form of primitive need. (It is, after all, what many tribes do, too.) We don't know, but it calmed her completely. She stopped wanting this around 13 months.

All babies are unique, of course, but they all have their triggers for uneasiness, whether it's being scared the first time they see an animal or wanting only one parent's attention or feeling colicky or having sudden hunger or falling or loud noises or a parent leaving the room or getting a cut or bruise, etc.

The thing that's crucial in all the above situations is having that tribal presence and caretaking. The first year is pretty intense in that regard. It's the most intense year of the child-parent relationship, and the most work. If a couple is not ready to do all THAT, then they should put off having children until they are – or they will be neglectful and resentful, and start the relationship on a bad footing that could potentially never be corrected. If a couple is ready for it, enjoy it!

The Booby

I'm not the first to say that breast milk is the miracle fluid. It is loaded with nutrients and immune-system boosters. Babies need the booby in their first year – not store-bought replacements – and babies get great comfort on the boob. No matter how restless they are, once they start suckling, their whole demeanor calms down and they get that relaxed face of utter bliss. We've all seen it. It's a lovely sight to see!

I hardly ever listen to "experts" (many of whom have never had children), but this is one thing they almost get right. I say "almost" because the experts say a baby should be breast-fed for the first year, but most babies want the boob for two to four years. Kathryn wanted it (and got it) for the first three years. In tribes, the babies often take the boob until age five, and I think this is a natural inclination to get primo nutrition and comfort. It gives the babies that WOW factor about their world. At the very least, moms should be ready to breast-feed for the first year.

Before I go further, there are two very important subjects that must be tackled, pertaining to children's bodies and rights: vaccination and circumcision.

Don't Vaccinate

Vaccination is a highly controversial subject, but if we take the long-term health and rights of our children seriously, we shouldn't vaccinate. It's simply too dangerous.

There are, of course, two strongly opposing sides to the vaccination argument. But both sides do AGREE on the following important facts:

1) that vaccination can occasionally cause major long-term health issues or even death in some cases
2) that vaccines do contain harmful chemicals
3) that vaccinations don't always work and, in fact, that they sometimes CAUSE the disease they are trying to prevent
4) that autism rates in kids have skyrocketed more than 10-fold (some say 40-fold) since the widespread introduction of vaccines in the 1960s
5) that over $2.7 billion has been awarded by courts and governments in the U.S. to families suffering from the consequences of vaccinations since 1989
6) that some diseases that vaccinations are aimed at (polio, diphtheria, etc.) have been eradicated in the U.S.
7) that most of the diseases that vaccinations target are actually not harmful for long-term health in almost all cases (chicken pox, mumps, measles, etc.), and the few cases in which these diseases do become serious, it is because the parents live in unsanitary conditions and don't get medical help for the kids

These are the facts that the two sides AGREE on. Is that not enough agreement to warrant non-vaccination? I think so.

What the above seven points make clear is that the danger to long-term health from GETTING vaccinations is greater than NOT GETTING vaccinations. This is the primary issue that objective parents should consider and decide on.

The two sides disagree on whether autism can be linked to vaccinations, but the pro-vaccination side admits that they don't know why autism has skyrocketed, and they say, incredibly, that it CAN'T be vaccinations – though no studies have been able to conclusively predict the affect of the toxic chemicals used in vaccinations, including thimerosal, aluminum and formaldehyde.

With the potential danger of vaccination being serious debilitation of our children (autism, anaphylaxis, long-term seizures, coma, or brain damage) and the potential diseases that might be caught by not vaccinating are virtually harmless in sanitary households near medical help, I cannot see why any parent would choose to expose their children to vaccination chemicals.

As a side-note, one thing the pro-vaccination side rarely talks about is that it wasn't vaccinations that caused the major shift in disease infections in the United States between 1850 and 1970. It was the biological revolution in understanding of germs, which led to much better sanitary conditions and clean water across America, bringing down infections by a factor of 10 for almost all diseases, except polio.

Parents could've made a case for giving only the polio vaccine to their children from the 1950s to the 1970s in the U.S., but polio has now been wiped out in America, so the dangers of the vaccine far outweigh any potential benefit.

In my opinion, the vaccination revolution hasn't been a revolution at all. It's been a war on children's bodies and rights for more than a half-century – except for the polio vaccine for three decades. Our sanitation, clean water and top-notch health care make current vaccinations a health hazard – not a health wonder.

I think that any infant who could somehow understand all of the above information and be able to speak would say, "No thank you. I think I'll remain clean."

With the above in mind, I think it is the right of the child to not be vaccinated.

Don't Circumcise

Circumcision has been around for millennia, and we're still not sure how it started, but it was picked up by many major religious groups, including Jews, Christians and Muslims, so about one-third of the Earth's population has had their genitals cut at birth or soon afterward.

Circumcision is predominantly an elective procedure – meaning, of course, that it has no medical or health purpose. It has been a cultural/religious tradition, with some believing (falsely) that it is more sanitary or believing (correctly) that it will hinder sexual satisfaction when the child reaches puberty. The first reason is ignorance, and the second reason is maliciousness. Many parents simply think that it's something that's supposed to be done. I hope those parents will now think twice.

Circumcision is a primitive procedure that violates kids' rights to their own bodies. I'm not saying, of course, that loving parents set out to violate their children's rights. Many parents simply don't give it much thought and have succumbed to tradition. But it is time to stop this mutilation of our children's midsection. It has no medical purpose. It is, frankly, barbaric – especially the cutting of the infant girl's clitoris, which is a savage attempt to keep her from having pleasure during intercourse.

I've tackled two somber but necessary subjects, so now it's time to get back to the more enjoyable aspects of parenting.

Home Base

When I say us Care-Friends need to watch ALL THE TIME, I'm not exaggerating too much. The parent is the baby's "home base". We are their sun, and their life revolves around us. They watch to see where we are. At first they crawl only a small distance from us, and then further and further, and eventually out of site, but not out of hearing range.

If we are paying attention, we have an "instinct" for where they are and how they are feeling. We KNOW if any discomfort is setting in, and should respond immediately, picking them up and soothing and chatting. When I say "instinct", I don't really mean that word, because adult humans don't really have instincts. We have years of experience that we put into our subconscious, so we automatically sense when things are good or not so good. Mothers seem to be especially aware of their babies' sounds and moods and looks.

Our lives change in that first year as a Care-Friend. We've added a permanent friend to our close circle – a very dependent close friend. We are raising a potentially amazing human and we are ever watchful that they are safe and feel warm and gooey about their world and us. We are their proxy. They aren't old enough to protect themselves and get things for themselves, so we are doing everything for them that they would do if they could. We are their home base.

One of my close friends once said (with tongue in cheek), "Yeah, we're pretty much slaves for that first year."

My friend was kidding of course, but I like to think of it more as benevolent butlers and maids who are always in attendance, getting to experience first-hand that giggling, fat bundle of curiosity who looks you directly in the eye, almost as if he's saying, "I love you, and THANK YOU FOR BEING THERE FOR ME!"

Inoculating the Home

I'm not saying anything new when I say that we should all "baby-proof" our homes with a new infant about, but I will stress how utterly important this is both for the baby and for US.

When babies begin to crawl, they will do things, many things: climb, touch, turn over, drop, start trying to stand, throw things and much more. These are not BAD things they are trying to do to our home – just THINGS they are doing. They are still at least a year away from having some knowledge of "bad". They're simply trying things out and getting a feeling for where the heck they are and what it's all about. I probably get my most upset when I see parents get upset or impatient with babies. A baby has no idea what he's doing yet, and we can only get upset with people who KNOW what they are doing.

We did the basic things to "inoculate" our home: put away or lock up all the breakable or poisonous objects; put away or lock up "inky" things that make marks; round off or put cushions over sharp edges on tables or other things; put away tiny objects and valuables – or they may be swallowed and pooped out the following day!

Baby-proofing the home gives us piece of mind, so that our Watchman status doesn't have to be a Centurion status, worrying all the time about danger. If our baby does break something or gets hurt badly, it's probably our fault for not thinking ahead and being The Watchman.

Many parents, including myself, put plastic and aluminum pans and other non-harmful items in the lower kitchen cabinets. The baby will find these ASAP after beginning to crawl and have many play days (home becomes a clanky orchestra).

The "clanky orchestra" stage is where the parent truly begins to understand what NOISE is. Before our children can understand how to control themselves a bit around 2 years old, they make noise and they LOVE noise, starting at about 6 months old. Noise is the exciting world talking back to them. It's ironic that we usually have babies when we've finally gotten to a stage in our lives where we don't like noise anymore. Ha! Nature has a sense of humor.

If we don't prepare for this noise ahead of time and get comfortable with just how intense it can be, it can be a very difficult mental disruption. The good thing is that the "orchestra" only lasts for about 12 months – "only" about 12 months. There's lots of noise after that stage, but nothing like The Clanky Year!

You can moderate the noise a bit by having things around that are a little less noisy for them to play with (plastic), but I found the best thing to do is just welcome the noise and enjoy their loud playfulness during this brief "garage band" stage. I liked to put on my own music at a high volume and try to enjoy it as much as possible while the baking pans were being turned into ear-splitting cymbals a few feet away.

Without too much planning for the newborn, many parents get the above Watchman role completely right or nearly right, paving the way for a potentially very happy, healthy one-year-old who feels at home in her new world and ready to conquer it.

But then …

But then many of those same parents feel it's time to start controlling their child and telling the child to do things she doesn't want to do or NOT do things she has every right to do – like be quiet or share your toys or don't pour your own milk or don't leave the room or eat all your food or don't touch things in the store or don't play with that (something YOU left out) or go to sleep (when they have the right to decide when they want to sleep).

I call "controlling" The X Factor. It's the "X" that cancels out kids' freedom of choice. But we don't have to control, and we shouldn't control, and we can stop doing it. In the next two chapters, I'll talk about getting away from "control" and using Leverage, with young kids and older kids, so everybody's rights are honored.

Chapter Twelve

The Co-Pirate
Our Co-Piloting Role as Baby Goes Vertical

Imagine waking up this morning like 30-year-old Claire coming out of her coma – or like infants and young Claire after their first year of life.

You know nothing, except a few faces and some objects around you. Everything is brand-spanking new. You can't understand anything yet. Even the glowing numbers on the bedside clock are not numbers; they are just beams of fascinating light. You have no idea about the concepts of "light" or "numbers" or "time". You have no idea about words, which are simply concepts expressed by humans relating to things in the universe.

You have no idea about hot and cold, smooth and rough, high and low, sweet and sour, food and not-food, angry and happy, tall and short, good and bad, boy and girl, safety and danger, fast and slow, thick and thin, sharp and dull, words, math, marriage, grammar, books, hair, insects, animals, the universe, genitals, the brain, digestion, sex, the lower back, cars, salt, water, candles, trees, engines, electronics, the Internet, fitness, friends, family, wars, disease, psychology, identity – nothing!

You are tabula rasa (a blank slate), with only a certain sort-of WAY about you, which is indeed unique for all of us when we are born. (I'm always fascinated by the difference in personalities of newborns in a maternity ward. Must be some sort of natural wiring that makes us all different from the very beginning.)

For a while, like the lower animals, you don't even know that you exist. You don't know what existence is.

And yet!

NASA, We Have Liftoff

And yet, within just 10 years or so, baby Claire and all other kids understand to some degree or full degree everything in the list above without anyone's help. And they know 100,000+ things on top of that. What an awesome mind!

But even after one year of life, kids still don't know they are SOMEONE yet. They don't know that they are something that's called ALIVE. They don't know that there is such a thing as death. They are simply captivated by the simple things – what they see and hear and feel and taste and smell around them. And they MOVE towards those things with a vengeance!

As the famous former educator John Holt (the "unschooler") said: "The human animal is a learning animal." Holt understood that children learn best when left to their own devices and NOT in a forced "education" setting. As he said, the world IS their education.

By about the age of 10, without a spec of outside organized education, a child will learn all alone everything necessary (language, math, reading, logical constructions, morals, judgment, organization, music, writing, art, chess, dance, constructing, designing, etc.) to govern her life for the rest of her life – and perform up to 90% of the jobs on Earth. And with a few personally chosen short classes, she could do 95% of the jobs on Earth. With more of those personal classes, she could do ANY job on Earth, outside of labor that requires physical strength that is beyond her capacity.

All by the age of 10 – and all by herself, if she so chooses. She's a rocket ship.

But kids have to start somewhere. That "start" on the learning/life Path is around the age of one. They won't start saying "I" until about the age of four, but that won't stop them from their pirate exploration – a survival-mode discovery mission that puts Columbus and other Renaissance adventurers to shame in the child's pure breadth of adventure and accumulation of facts of life. They have a whole world to discover and figure out. EVERYTHING is new.

Their minds form new concepts at a sizzling pace. To get a bit technical again, a "concept" is a unique imprint on our minds that represents two or more similar things in reality. It is formed via logic in human brains by looking at the facts of reality and grouping two or more similar things into an imprint – like "trees" or "moms" or "cars" or "tables" or "fast" or "hot", etc. We encounter these things, and we form concepts for them, many times after hearing someone else use the concepts. All of our brains are automatically wired to do this, if left alone. We are the only animal wired to do this.

Us humans use words to express our concepts, and we can understand these words or express them through a number of actions, such as speaking or hand movements (sign language) or touch (Helen Keller) or sound units (Morse Code). If we didn't have concepts, we couldn't have words, and if we didn't have words, we couldn't communicate and think on an extremely high level, like we do.

It is the rational brain (free will and concept formation) that greatly separates us from the lower species, and all of us (barring a mental disorder) have about equal ability in using our rational brains, including children. Watch a child learn language (concept formation) at a break-neck pace. Watch a child pick up an iPad at the age of 2 and figure our organization, movement and shortcuts within just hours, understanding cause and effect. At 18 months, they can group objects of the same color or shape, or they can see that square things don't go through round holes, conceptually understanding dimension and color.

Claire's mind will notice that there are many things and that most things are different but that some things are similar and there are a lot of those similar things (tree, table, chair, light, grass, shoe, picture, milk, feet, etc.). She will hear people give sounds (words) to these things and start using the sounds herself.

Then she'll move on to higher-level concepts that are not actual THINGS in reality but that are human words for groups of things or actions or qualities or states of being or associations (good, bad, long, short, mean, nice, high, low, old, young, hot, cold, people, society, community, government, death, life, fast, slow, of, that, those, the, many, taxes, money (dollars and coins exist, but "money" Is a highor concept that denotes dollars and coins and other forms of "money"). These are known as "higher-level concepts" – not readily available to our five senses. When I stop and think about this human ability, I'm always in awe.

Claire and other kids are oblivious to this lightning-fast concept-formation and word formation that they are doing, but they do it virtually perfectly every time.

And they need full freedom to gather this info on their own Path, doing it on their own time schedule, not OURS – to find their own meaning and be self-full. They will use their free will to choose what they want to explore and learn. They will integrate all that info, correcting mistakes as they go along (like adults) – such as thinking that all coffee is hot, but later finding that some coffee is served cold, or thinking all birds can fly and then learning about ostriches. They correct that immediately because they like to be in tune with reality, to be logical and connected.

Our toddlers learn all of the above on their pirate Paths, in every-day experiences as they go vertical and move horizontal in their quest for fun and adventure and understanding. Us Care-Friends can certainly enjoy identifying things for our kids, like dog or car or phone, or even correcting them occasionally when they get something wrong – but in most cases of concept-formation (words), kids get the name of everything around them by simply listening and watching. Amazing!

No Leverage in the First Vertical Year

The 12 months that our children are 1 year old are most likely the primo months for lifelong habits. By the time they turn 2, they should already understand all of these things from us:

1) They are free to explore a good Path.
2) There are limits on exploration (street, TV screen, parents' drinks, glass objects in stores, other kids' eyeballs, and so on …)
3) Cleaning up spills and other messes is FUN.
4) They can accomplish many things, including pouring the milk jug when it is low on milk, or even when it's got a lot of milk and mommy or daddy helps.
5) We like to talk with them and explain tons of things to them.
6) We like to carry them.
7) They are immensely loved and valuable to us.
8) We like to do things with them.
9) We are calm all the time with them.
10) They feel secure.

They are old enough to explore at this age but not really old enough to understand rules much, so using Leverage with them would be fruitless and mean. The key to this age is communication and personal contact and explanation and sharing of life.

They are utterly fascinated with absolutely everything at this age, including spills. They are mesmerized while watching a paper towel absorb a milk spill. They want to do THAT themselves. We should let them handle the paper towel. That's where habits begin.

They will hardly ever clean up perfectly in the beginning, but of course it doesn't matter. We can finish up or help them, if they don't mind. (If we want to help them, we must always ask for their OK, no matter how excruciatingly slow they are. We must honor their rights.)

The important point is that they no longer see spills as something that someone else takes care of or something "bad". Spills are something THEY take care of automatically, and spills just happen. After several spills, their habit is SET. You will rarely have to remind them afterward to clean up after themselves. They LIKE doing it. By the time my daughter was 2, she would race me (her idea) to see who could clean a spill faster. Fun! And she got good at avoiding spills, especially when the novelty wore off and she wasn't so crazy about cleaning them up anymore.

Too many parents, unfortunately, don't let the "spill" scene or other such scenes play out the child's way –1-year-olds can be glacially slow at cleaning up at first. Too many parents get impatient during this time and interfere with the cleaning scene because the parent wants it cleaned up quickly or because the parent knows that the child won't do a great job. The parent wants to CONTROL the situation, even though there's nothing that should be controlled.

Co-Pirates

There is nothing to be controlled because, like adults, the child is the pilot of his pirate ship, and we, really, are simply the co-pilots – or perhaps Co-Pirates. We are along for the glorious ride and occasionally, when asked, help out with the piloting.

Seeing ourselves as Co-Pirates during the toddler stage – and even throughout their entire childhood adventure – puts our Care-Friend role again into its proper perspective on being the friend and co-adventurer, instead of controller or guide. It helps us in these Lightning Moments to remember that their pirate life is about them and want they want, and NOT about what we want.

We are simply their adoring Co-Pirates – for childhood and for life.

The Can-Do Spirit

The Lightning Moments are when we should remind ourselves that our kids are quite capable of taking care of themselves and their messes and other things – perhaps not at our pace, but is that pace REALLY that important? Is it really necessary for us to impose our values of "fast" and "cleaned well" on our children in these moments, thereby sending a message to them that it is not THEIR values in the moment that are important – and putting a block between our good relationship.

This Lightning Moment, like all Lightning Moments, is a responsibility-builder, creating good character – and, more importantly, the pirate actually has the RIGHT to clean up his own mess, if he likes. They absolutely love that you don't interfere with them, and that you also enjoy being with them and perhaps helping them if they need it. With my daughter, she wanted to try to figure out which cartoon character a certain spill on the floor or counter resembled the most. Creativity abounded!

This same rule of honoring our child should play out all the time, including, for example, when they want to use their hands or utensils at home or at a restaurant to feed themselves. We should honor their right to do so. They want to be self-determined and self-sufficient and self-full. That is their survival mode they're born with. To continually interfere with this independence creates kids who eventually think strongly, as they get older, that you should be doing everything for them, and they learn to not be independent. And, frankly, why wouldn't they start believing we are their servant, if we continually do things for them that they can and want to do for themselves?

On top of all that, the toddler begins to not feel capable because, frankly, we are showing that they aren't capable in those situations. This can have negative longterm effects on their self-esteem and free will, not to mention making them obedient, instead of independent. It also tells them that they are not in charge of their lives, and that somebody outside them will always be in control of them and be telling them what to do and what not to do. Frankly, it's a recipe for raising obedient children, at the least, and spoiled brats, at the worst. As children and as adults, we should not be obedient to others. We should value independence always!

Getting back to the spilled milk, if our toddler tries to walk away from it, we should lead them back, "Hey Claire, you left a spill on the floor, baby, so let's go back and clean it up, and then we can watch 'Dora The Explorer'". Have the paper towel in hand and maybe begin the cleanup, allowing her to finish. If you remain happy and engaged about the task, she will be happy and engaged. No Leverage necessary. We just communicate clearly and stay involved and pick them up when necessary and help them take care of things.

By letting them take care of themselves at age one, including getting toys out of the livingroom (with our help, if necessary), we watch our kids gain confidence in themselves and confidence in our thoughtful caretaking and an understanding of good rules. It imbues trust between Care-Friend and child for the rambunctious Twos – and beyond.

So because we have honored their right to run their lives, they feel good about us Co-Pirates. They feel like their lives are THEIR lives, and they want to share those lives with those who have honored their lives. So when they go down their good Paths, they enjoy us watching them and being a part of those Paths with them. When they go down bad Paths, they now trust us enough to listen and eventually change to the good Path under our Oak Tree, whether we are just communicating with them or using our Leverage.

The reason they trust us is because we have proven and shown that we won't try to control them. It is the benevolent relationship of Pirate and Co-Pirate.

Chapter Thirteen

Leverage (Two)
We Got the Power

This is the longest chapter in the book. I'll be going through a lot of examples of raising kids and their Paths of Least Resistance and how we use the things we own (our power) to ensure GOOD Paths. Let's remember, though, that power can be good, very good, but absolute power corrupts absolutely. So we must be fair!

I'll give examples of how Care-Friends (as Watchmen) use the things they own as Leverage to stop bad Paths in their kids in every single Lightning Moment of the budding friendship. Those five "things" are: **money, things, caretaking, love, communication** – the same five things we temporarily remove from all friendships in which a friend is violating our rights or disrespecting us with a bad Path.

I'll also be dispelling a few mistaken perceptions about child-rearing – such as "sharing" and saying "No" and "tantrums". And I'll talk about how humor is a NECESSITY for raising good kids and having fun with them.

This chapter is full of examples of daily life with children, and how we remain the Happy Oak Tree using Leverage fairly to get good Paths.

I'll be explaining two different scenarios on each example – one for new parents, who haven't had kids or have infants and are starting parenthood fresh, and one for parents who already have 2- to 17-year-old kids and may have to use Leverage a little more because their children are not used to the Happy Oak Tree and rights.

New parents get the chance to honor their children's rights from the very beginning, using "easy" Leverage as the Happy Oak Tree. Your kids never have to be "fixed" because you're starting early. They start out "clean", with no bad habits of walking over others or ever having been controlled by you or others.

You have been or will be the ever-present Watchman during their infancy, building full trust and communication by the time they are 1 year old. And you have been their fun and loving Co-Pirate during the toddler stage, honoring their freedom to run their own lives as they begin moving around their new world. You have shown that you care and will always care about them and their rights, so they have absolutely no reason not to trust you when you begin to use Leverage and set the proper rules for an abiding relationship as their pirate mind explores Paths.

What I mean by "easy" is that your new pirates will trust your use of Leverage, which will be accepted quickly because they have not been jaded by bad communication or bad rules or helicoptering. You don't have to stay "strong" for hours, as parents with older kids may have to do sometimes while introducing Leverage to "fix" their kids. In fact, as I said before, you'll rarely even have to use Leverage with children who completely trust your actions.

But on those rare occasions, you still will have to be a Happy Oak Tree using Leverage, because young children take several years to conceptually grasp that their pirate Paths must not interfere with other pirate Paths of those around them.

When we raise kids free starting at birth, using Leverage usually only takes a few minutes – or even just the mention of the Leverage that will be used brings about a good Path of Least Resistance. We've established our friendly but unbending ways, and we have earnestly tried to be a true and communicative friend to them. They trust us and they LIKE us. We have made it clear that we honor their good Path and that we have our own good Path, and we are walking those pirate Paths nearby each other in joyful bliss.

Parents who already have older kids can get to this same stage of respect and trust in just a matter of weeks or months, depending on your confidence – and your kids' detecting that confidence. Once you've gotten to the good Path stage, you will also rarely have to use Leverage to ensure good Paths and a respect for rights.

I'll be using examples of situations that almost all parents encounter with kids aged 2 through 17. During these 16 years of glorious adventure by our kids, we will be the loving Oak Tree who uses Leverage properly, regularly watching out for our rights and others' rights as our pirates explore their new world with boundaries – so we can all be self-full and have full meaning.

Here are the rules of being the Happy Oak tree using Leverage:

1) Be in the moment, staying calm and not losing your temper
2) Use humor, fun-sarcasm and incredulity (disbelief) to get their attention

3) Act immediately when a Lightning Moment occurs
4) Keep the context of the child's age and understanding always in mind
5) Never apologize for being right ("I'm sorry, but ...")
6) Remind yourself that you are talking to a dear friend
7) Remind yourself that your dear friend MUST learn boundaries from YOU
8) Remind yourself that you may have to be the Oak Tree many times before your child understands the rule and respects you and rights
9) Be prepared to escalate if necessary – using more than one of your Leverages in a Lightning Moment if one Leverage isn't working
10) Be the Oak tree no matter where you are at the moment – you are right, so other people's opinion of your actions do not matter, because your relationship with your dear child-friend matters MOST
11) Use facts and ONLY facts all the time
12) Don't be afraid to pass judgment on your friend, so that you stay strong
13) Be happy with your own life, so you can be the Happy Oak Tree
14) Remind yourself that the Lightning Moment will pass and all will be great
15) Pat yourself on the back for a job well-done and creating an awesome kid

The Incredible Twos

By the age of about 2, children have more confidence in their bodies and movements, and the world is no longer entirely new to them. They feel more comfortable with their surroundings. At this age, they still cannot introspect and understand who they are, so they are almost always in a pirate GO mode.

It is this "wild" age that seems to confound and upset many parents, leading to the common misnomer "The Terrible Twos". As I said earlier in the book, it's actually "The Incredible Twos". They are breaking out of those earlier shells of misunderstanding and confusion and perplexity and newness.

If Year One is about being the Watchman, and Year Two is about being the Co-Pirate and letting them explore and handle their own messes, Year Three (when they are 2) is about letting them go and setting boundaries as an Oak Tree – ALWAYS. We parents should welcome the

Twos as a time of getting down to "rights" boundaries. It sets the guidelines and actions for the rest of their lives. If you get your Happy Oak Tree down well here, you'll almost cruise through the rest of your child's growth, as long as you always remain the Oak Tree.

Ages 2 and 3 – The NOISE Years

Kids are loud. They like loud. They thrive on loud. They live for LOUD!

Adults don't. So it's almost like looking at aliens when our kids get louder and louder. (Ha!) It can drive an adult absolutely batty if we don't set fair and sturdy boundaries on noise levels around us and others.

I suppose noise is new to kids and it is a confirmation of the world around them being there and being real – and that THEY are real. Us adults like to introspect a lot on our lives, our friends, our goals, what we'll cook, etc., so our thinking usually needs mostly peace and quiet. Kids are generally much more involved with DOING something right now and right LOUD. It is sort of fascinating – especially since the kids don't consider what they are doing as LOUD.

We can't hold a grudge that they are so different, so we simply have to ensure that their noise does not interfere with our right to occasional quiet or semi-quiet – that they understand that we and others have a right to our peace. Here's an example of how to use Leverage to handle "loud" with a 2- or 3-year-old.

At the Restaurant

Our 2 (or 3) year old wants to bang the silverware and salt shaker and other things at the restaurant while in the high chair. His 4-year-old sister Charlotte is with us. We've already explained to Charlie before we go in the restaurant that we can't be loud in the restaurant because it's somebody else's place and they want it to be quiet. We explained nicely but firmly that if any of us gets loud (including adults) and won't be quiet that that person will have to go outside the restaurant until they quiet down.

It's good to remind children that rules apply equally to adults. (My daughter, around the age of 4, used to get a kick out of saying, "Um, excuse me, but your movie is so loud that I can't concentrate. Um, you know the rules!" I would say "oops" and turn down the volume. We would both get smiles on our faces and she would walk back out. SHE was being her own Happy Oak Tree.)

When we have more than one child, it's important to explain potential predicaments to all the children before doing something or going someplace, and explain what that might mean for everyone involved, and get their acceptance of the situation before taking them.

In the restaurant situation, we explain to Charlotte beforehand that if we have to take Charlie outside the restaurant that she would have to go with us, if we are by ourselves as a parent at the restaurant. We get Charlotte's OK on this first, to honor her rights.

It's critical to prepare everyone for any eventuality always, out of respect for their time and rights. Forewarnings and fair communication are trust-builders! It shows that we always have their rights and importance to us at the top of our minds. And it shows that we are so in charge of things and want things to go so smoothly that we think ahead of time about everything and everyone.

So, Charlie simply won't stop banging things or yelling at interesting things in the restaurant. He's in his own world. After we calmly explain to him one more time about what we talked about, he continues being loud soon after. As we stand up with calmness, we say to Charlie, "OK, love, looks like you're not going to be quiet in these people's restaurant, so we need to go outside for a bit to get quiet."

We look at Charlotte and say, "Sorry, honey, but gotta go outside for a few minutes. I'll get you a little something extra after lunch to make up for it. Thanks." We are the ones causing her inconvenience, so, in my book, we owe her a little something. This kind of constant fairness imbues such trust in kids that it's off the charts.

We shouldn't be surprised that Charlie can't yet control himself like us, so we can't be one bit angry at his momentary lapse. It's a natural part of growth in young kids. We should be matter-of-fact – like we were just taking a phone call outside – even if he is screaming. I'm actually quite sympathetic of what Charlie is going through. He doesn't understand why he can't have full-blown fun! But rules are rules. And he'll get it soon enough.

As we unbuckle Charlie, he gets upset and starts squirming and possibly screaming. The other patrons won't mind the temporary screaming because they see that we're in the middle of handling the noise problem. And, frankly, it doesn't matter what the other patrons are thinking about our parenting if we are in the process of ensuring that everyone's rights are being considered, which we are.

The one time I had to do this with Kathryn, I apologized to the patrons around me, but they were all smiling knowingly and said, "Oh no, we understand, please don't apologize." Though they would've been rightly angry if I didn't handle the situation quickly.

The Leverage in this situation is "things": the restaurant, the silverware, the salt shaker, the environment. We are removing this "fun" place from Charlie. To be a little technical about this, we are not initiating coercion against Charlie. HE initiated (unknowingly) the violation of other people's space, so we are responding as the Happy Oak Tree with the force necessary to end the violation.

If an adult friend made a big ruckus at a our table in a restaurant and thought it was funny and wouldn't stop, then our only option would be to pay our part of the tab quickly and simply walk out, which I had to do once in my 20s because of a half-drunk guy.

Because we are Charlie's loving Care-Friend until his rationality allows him to understand rules fully and make the right decision at the table, we have the right to remove him from the trouble spot. (Wish I could've done this with the 20-something guy many years ago!)

We get Charlie out of the chair and outside and are walking around chatting about the things around us with him in our arms, and he begins to calm down. He wants to get down and walk around, and we let him do it safely. Yes, our food is getting cold inside the restaurant. Such are the Lightning Moments of parenting! Which is more important: warm food or helping our child learn the proper Path of Least Resistance by being his Happy Oak Tree? In the long run, we'll have a lot more warm meals if we are sturdy right NOW.

After a few minutes, we tell Charlie that we're ready to go back in and eat some good food. Ask him if he's ready. As we re-enter, we remind him in a loving (but steady) voice that everybody has to be pretty quiet and that we'll have to come back outside if he's loud again. He gets it as well as a 2- or 3-year-old can get it. We shouldn't be holding grudges when we eat our cold food. We should remind ourselves that these things will happen for a short while and are definitely WORTH it in the long run.

(At this stage of Kathryn's life, I usually warned servers at restaurants that I might have to step outside with her if she got too loud. I only ended up having to do it once, but the servers were always terrific and grateful that I mentioned it. Everybody loves good communication!)

The tone of voice in the above scenario and all scenarios with children is crucial. We should talk to them as equals, as if they are 30-year-old Claire reverting back to childhood traits for a while – as if Claire had been the one at the table making the noise. (Would be VERY hard to carry her out!) We should ask ourselves if we would be proud of how we treated Claire or Charlie in this short episode of their lives. Our kids are our budding friends, our equals in individual rights. We should always think about their mental context in each situation, and give them the benefit of the doubt.

Charlie will probably only do this one or two times if you are the Happy Oak Tree with your Leverage. Two-year-olds have good memories of how you handled a certain situation, and Charlie will remember the restaurant rule from now on. But if he's stubborn or you weren't the Oak Tree in his first two years of life, he might "try" you a couple more times.

Your solution is simple. Keep being the Oak Tree and NEVER EVER bend in a Lightning Moment. If you bend, you lose and have to start over again.

If you do bend, don't fret too much. You just lapsed in a weak moment. Have a good talk with yourself and remind yourself how awesome you can be and how you love your kids too much to let them walk over you or anyone else – and then jump right back in prepared for the next Lightning Moment. He will come around on the fourth or fifth or sixth time you use your Leverage. And you'll be ecstatic!

A very dear friend of mine had a difficult time being the Happy Oak Tree. She had a rough childhood and her self-esteem was low and she didn't want her kids to have a tough childhood, so she was overly lenient when her children took the bad Path, running over her and others. She tried talking to them, but it didn't work. She took their toys away, and it made their rebellion worse. She occasionally hit them, and made things horrible. She began to get depressed and have occasional eruptions of temper in the home and even in stores.

We had become acquaintances when my daughter was five, and she asked me one day why my daughter never did the things her children did. I explained to her the things I'm explaining in this book. She didn't believe it at first. She thought that making kids FREER would be a catastrophe.

Eventually, she started letting go of the false rules and the helicoptering, and she began to be the Oak Tree and started using her Leverage fairly. It took her about two years to get full confidence in herself and her new approach, but she finally nailed it and became positively giddy. Her kids are terrific now and have been my daughter's longtime friends.

I think it's good to celebrate the Lightning Moment victories, to remind ourselves of hard work done well and how much our friendship with our children means to us. We should celebrate when Charlie becomes a fun-loving and semi-quiet person in the restaurant, where we can always look forward to a great time without hassle.

The thing that I found that gave me great comfort is that I could be a good Oak Tree and that I could pull out that Oak Tree whenever necessary and wherever necessary – whether it was with a child or an adult. It's very comforting to know you can do that. It calms you down in all situations. You know what your rules are.

Other People's Kids

One prickly situation you may run into often is being around your adults friends who did not raise their kids free and weren't Oak Trees with boundaries for their kids – and they get angry with their kids a lot and let their kids make a lot of noise in restaurants or take any bad Path they want to take..

The way I see it is we have two options: 1) leave or 2) ask the parent if they would mind if you can be the Care-Friend and picked up their noise-making child and walk outside. This makes some moms and dads pretty mad, obviously, because you've just implicitly told them that they are not taking care of their child. But, surprisingly, many parents are glad you asked and tell you it's OK – frankly because they want to keep on ignoring their child, or they just don't know how to be a Happy Oak Tree.

For young kids who came to our house with their parents, I always explained to the new visiting adults and kids how our house was about freedom and not violating others' rights. The usual response I got from the kids was, "OK." And from the adults, it was something like, "Yeah, of course, you can tell my kids to do anything. It's your house."

So, I would take the parents for their word. Either my daughter or I would tell new kids what the rules were and to have all the fun in the world, as long as they didn't interfere with someone else doing the same. All of the kids understood my daughter's Oak Tree and my Oak Tree within one or two visits, and they had a great time together, playing and honoring each other's rights.

One quick point on this is your explanation when the new visitors arrive. In a fun but firm voice and face, you explain that if someone can't play well by not honoring others or being mean-spirited, then they would have to leave.

In my daughter's early childhood, this almost happened once with a 7-year-old boy. But, after talking with him one last time, he finally got the Oak Tree and stopped harassing my daughter and the other kids. And after that, he was terrific each time he came over. And he always knew that the result of any further violations of rights would mean his parents would have to take him home.

After several visits by the boy, the father told me and Kathryn once that the boy seemed to be "calmer" and more fun after leaving our house. THIS is what the Happy Oak Tree and leverage does for kids.

As Care-Friends in charge of ensuring that we and our loved ones never have our rights or respect trampled on, we sometimes MUST stay confident when the Lightning Moment of a bad Path means someone would have to leave. But it usually doesn't come to that with kids who see and sense that your Oak Tree will not bend – and that the ideas of rights and respectfulness in your house are just as real and solid as the majestic tree itself.

The TV

The TV seems to be a particular bane of many households with children, and yet the TV is one of the easiest Leverages you have. All you have to do if kids insist on not honoring the volume levels, even after you've communicated with them nicely, is simply unplug it and put the cord someplace private (electricity Leverage). They get the message very quickly. It is your property, and it is your space they are violating.

Modern TVs usually have numbers that come up on the screen for the volume level. That makes it easy to give fair rules on noise levels for kids. My daughter and I agreed that the good noise level for when I was working at home was "8" and for when I went to bed before her a "7" and for just during the day when I didn't care about noise, it could go all the way up to "20", though she usually kept it at about 12 because she didn't like to bother me too much. I asked her what she wanted MY volume levels to be for the TV when she was around, and she said she didn't really care. (My gawd, kids love noise!) I could tell that she loved that I was asking her for MY volume rules, because she first shouted out jokingly "ONE!" before finally saying she didn't care. Ha!

Everyone, including kids, occasionally forgets the volume level, so we just remind them about it and they say "oops, sorry" and the volume comes down quickly. But we can tell if a 3-year-old (or anyone else) is purposely not abiding by the volume rule. He is resentful when reminded or nonchalant about the whole thing and slowly turns down the volume – often not far enough. This doesn't seem to happen with free-raised kids, but other kids may test you.

If this is the case, even after you've nicely communicated your reasoning several times before and gotten an agreement from them about the volume, then the Lightning Moment has arrived. "OK, darling, I get it. You don't care about the noise right now or about my ears and about what we said about the noise. So here goes." (you unplug TV very casually)

When kids (or others) know they are breaking a good rule and don't care about it, frankly, there can be no discussion for a while, or the child (or other person) will sense your weakness. THEY know that YOU know they are breaking the rule, so if you talk instead of act, they see that, and they REMEMBER it for future reference and Paths of Least Resistance against you.

And the opposite happens if you DO act quietly and confidently and happily. You are seen as an Oak Tree who goes about your business of being happily self-full and won't put up with interference EVER. You show your understanding of what the child is doing by simply walking over to the TV cord and taking it off the TV, with perhaps a few parting words in a matter-of-fact voice, "When you think you can keep the sound down, Ethan, you can come talk to me. Thanks." Don't explain what you are doing. It's obvious. Let them see what you are doing and the confidence and ease with which you do it.

If you have many children and they are arguing about who gets to watch what on the TV, frankly, that is OK, as long as their arguing is at a noise level that doesn't bother you. They are learning about how to work things out. They may ask you to help them, and that is a good thing too (trust). They will learn about diplomacy and fairness with those types of disagreements.

All disagreements with kids (or anyone else) should be taken as a positive by all people. A verbal disagreement is simply two people saying "I disagree and we need to work something out". That is always good if both sides are being fair and not name-calling.

Tantrums Are Not Natural

For those who have raised free kids and had terrific communication and total involvement in their lives and no helicoptering or false rules, the child will immediately get it and tell you they'll keep the volume down. (In fact, it won't even get to the point where you have to use your electricity Leverage.)

But kids who are not raised with full individual rights to run their own lives will occasionally throw tantrums when their bad Path of Least Resistance is challenged – by a parent who does not have their full trust. Tantrums are NOT a natural part of child-raising. They should never occur. If they do, it means something has gone wrong in the Care-Friend/child relationship. There is a communication and trust breakdown – and the responsibility for that communication is always on the parent.

For parents in the process of fixing their relationship and honoring rights, any tantrum or yelling that occurs when you unplug the TV needs to be taken with a grain of salt by you. (This is hard for you at first, but hang in there!) You can even say something a bit funny and sarcastic as you're unplugging, like, "I hear ya, baby! It ain't easy watching TV when there's no electricity." This shows your control as the Happy Oak Tree and that you don't respond to threats – tantrums are threats. They are not primarily the child hurting. They are the child trying to hurt YOU – trying to get YOU to back off from their bad Path that they desperately want.

As hard as all of the above will be, do not take the advice of pediatricians and others who do not understand children's rights. They will tell you that you should abandon your child at this moment and walk away or go to another room and let them stew in their own anger. (Or they will horribly suggest that you should send your child to abandonment "Time-Out".) This is the worst thing you can do, and it tells the child that you don't love them – and that you own them.

Children throwing tantrums should never be abandoned. You should stay calmly nearby and wait for them to cool down. You can read a book or play games on your phone, if you like, but you should not take your presence away from a hurting child EVER. They aren't ready to talk yet and you aren't ready to talk yet, but your calm presence and insistence on still having fun while they blow off their steam shows you care enough to be with them but that you won't accommodate their bad Path. It also shows you're ready to work things out when they're done.

If your child decides himself or herself to rampage out of the room and leave you, then you must NOT follow. They may have decided to use abandonment of you as THEIR Leverage or they just don't want to be around you. Simply stay exactly where the altercation began and enjoy yourself until they return. If they eventually begin playing happily in another room, that is terrific. It means they GET your Oak Tree and the Leverage. You can now freely go about having fun anywhere you like.

Tantrums are one of the hardest Lightning Moments to handle. If you can handle these as the Happy Oak Tree, you can handle ANYTHING as a Care-Friend!

Free-raised kids don't throw tantrums. At least, I've never seen one. I would imagine there never will be such a thing – because they've gotten used to the Happy Oak Tree and total fairness and trust in the relationship from birth. Free-raised kids treat you as a mommy-friend or daddy-friend. It really doesn't occur to them that you would be unfair or have rules that don't make sense. After all, you've talked about everything up to this point in total acknowledgement of each other. They are tapped into you, and you are tapped into them

If you tell them nicely that the volume is so high that it is difficult for you to concentrate, (always good to be specific with kids) they will immediately reach for the remote control and lower the volume. They will usually say, "Is that good, mommy?" and you might say, "Yes, love, perfect. Thanks very much." And you both go on your happy way. Children around Happy Oak Trees LIKE to be your friend and to accommodate you – the way that you accommodate them on good Paths.

Tantrums are the result of helicoptering and bad rules and not having full respect for children's rights. In other words, they are, unfortunately, the parents' fault – though, ironically, it is the kids who are punished by parents during tantrums.

A tantrum is the sign of immense frustration on the child's part (though I've seen frustrated and angry adults throw tantrums). It means someone is feeling burdened by outside demands and "authority". It means that the channel of trust and communication between parent and child is turned off or muffled. It means the child does not respect the opinion or rules of the person who won't talk to them and respect them, and who tells them what to do all or most of the time – the person who doesn't allow them to pursue their own meaning in life and be self-full.

The tantrum child sees the TV cord next to you as you play on your phone. They see your calm use of Leverage. Once they settle down, you can ask them if they are ready to talk. You don't ask them if they are ready to "listen". That is acting like you are the teacher/preacher/authority who is being condescending. We would not ask a friend who was mad if they are "ready to listen". (THAT would make them madder, as it does children.) We would just simply say, "You ready to talk yet?" in a nice voice.

Once a tantrum child or any other child on a temporary bad Path sees your Happy Oak Tree's confident and fair use of Leverage one time or several times, they will alter their path and enjoy the TV at a respectful volume, like the rest of the family.

The above rules on using Leverage with older kids having tantrums works the same way, with one important change – you don't necessarily have to remain near them when they are having a fit. Because their rationality is in full gear and they know who they are and can make full choices themselves, you can calmly say to them as you're leaving the room with the TV cord: "Let me know when you're ready to talk."

Find Your Funny Bone and Don't Say "No!"

At a party I threw many years ago, an acquaintance of one of my friends was putting her dirty napkins down through the edges of the cushions of my couch while eating barbecue!! (that deserved two exclamation marks) I've never had the inclination to yell "No!" at my daughter or any other kids, but I felt like shouting "No!" at that woman – among other things.

What I ended up doing was getting the small trashcan from under the kitchen sink and taking it to the woman in front of 12 people and asking her if she would be a darling and take the napkins from between the cushions and put them in the trashcan. She turned bright red and did so. I got the look of death from her for the rest of the evening. (Miss Manners may have approved of my diplomacy!) When I looked up from the woman, many people in the room had huge grins and were nodding. Justice is a dish best served cold.

Humor isn't just the elixir of youth. It's also the grease of the good life and difficult situations, letting YOU know that you're in charge, and letting the WORLD know that you're in charge. With your funny bone as your secret "weapon" for handling virtually anything, you should never have to say "No" – in fact, outside of physical aggression against us, telling anyone "No" or "Don't" to stop them from doing something is condescending and authoritarian. This includes kids, too.

If a friend is drinking too much or our teenager is backing out of our driveway too fast or playing their music too loud or texting dangerously in the middle of heavy traffic or being rude to a service worker or someone is trying to tell our child what to do, we don't shout out "No" or "Don't". Condescension and anger rarely work.

But incredulity (disbelief) and humor almost always work.

"Bill, you sound like you just got out of the dentist chair. Can I get you a glass of orange juice or water?" ... "Anny! Do you see racetrack stripes on the driveway? Kids in the neighborhood. Slooooooow down please. Thanks!" ... "John, that's the person who took our order – um, NOT the one who put mayo on your burger." ... "Baby, if you're going to keep texting in this traffic, please text the undertaker."

If humor or incredulity don't work, then you can escalate tone and use Leverage. "Bill, you're getting a bit obnoxious. I'm going to have to leave, if you keep drinking." ... "Anny, if you and your accelerator continue your love affair coming out of the driveway, you'll have to park on the street from now on." ... "John, I'm going to have to step outside if you continue to harass this nice worker." ... "Please drop me off at the next corner, baby, since you can't stop texting. Thank you."

If you say the above calmly and firmly and will back up what you say with your actions, it gets almost everyone's attention, and you put an end to bad Paths. Usually, you can get it done with humor, but if not, time to escalate with Leverage. And we never said "No!" or "Don't". We honored the equality of the relationship.

We don't shout "No" at the friends (our teenager is our friend, too) in the above circumstances or any such circumstances. So, we shouldn't do it with our kid-friends either – whether they're about to take a giant glass of red Kool-Aid to the white couch ("Whoa, whoa, whoa, yo, yo, yo! Put those legs in reverse! Kool-Aid at the kitchen table only for a while, remember? Thanks.") or whether they are banging their plastic hammer on the TV screen ("Whoa, Ethan! Are my eyes REALLY seeing you hit my TV with your plastic hammer?! Please tell me they aren't. Darling, hammers are for hitting NAILS. Please feel free to go find a nail to hit. Thank you very much. Good luck. Go forth and prosper!" Humor and firmness wrapped in one.

Dontchya

The same rule applies to "Don't" in our lives – nearly all of the time. If someone is messing with us personally, then a good, solid "Don't!" is perfect. But there are much better and more respectful ways to get points across to everyone we are around who's on a bad Path in other situations.

Most of the time, we'll just say firmly, "Please stop" or "No thanks" or "I'm done, thanks" or "Don't want to discuss it anymore. I'm good."

Same goes for kids, even for three-year-olds grabbing candy on store shelves. (Wish I had a dime for every time I heard a parent shout, "Don't touch the candy!") There's nothing technically wrong with touching candy, with all those colors and good pictures on them. Heck, I do it TOO sometimes!

Parents are often concerned that their kids will mess up the candy or drop it on the floor, but those are good times to help them with cleanup. Or parents are concerned that the kids will insist on having the candy, but that means the parents weren't clear before going to the store about what they would get and not get for everyone in the family – and that the parents had a history of being the Oak Tree, so that the kids KNEW that the parents were serious.

The reason so many parents are caught in the "Don't" loop is that they unfortunately don't tap in to their kids' context of life in the moment. So the parents don't communicate well about situations the kids don't know how to handle yet. The parents haven't communicated perfectly what the rules of a situation are before the situation occurs – such as setting the simple ground rules for the grocery store.

Aren't you tired of saying "Don't"? Dontchya wanna stop?

Communicating well and being the Happy Oak Tree and respecting our children's rights to find their Paths of meaning prevent "Don'ts" from popping into our heads.

"Sorry" Seems to Be the Hardest Word

"Sorry" is important to say and to NOT say.

When we screw up with adult friends, we apologize, and the same goes for kids. It should be sincere and immediate when we know we've done wrong. And we should use the word "sorry" or "apologize" and not try to skirt around our mess-up by trying to explain that we were busy and forgot or give some other rationalization.

To not apologize when we screw up ruins our credibility and wrecks our attempts at Leverage in the moments when we try to be the Happy Oak Tree. We can't be Happy Oak Trees in Lightning Moments if we aren't Honest Oak Trees about everything. Kids don't expect us to be perfect, but they DO expect us to own-up when we're not, just like our adults friends.

A good friend told me once, "I don't mind so much that restaurants mess up my orders. That happens. It's when they don't apologize and FIX it that bothers me!"

Exactly!

Kathryn once asked me to not let one of her friends play with her toys when Kathryn wasn't around, because the friend didn't treat the toys right and wouldn't put them back where they belong. I said OK. But a month later, I completely blitzed this promise, and Kathryn was pretty darn upset with me – especially considering that her friend AGAIN didn't put the toy back. I apologized and said I definitely wouldn't do that again and would definitely remember. I never forgot again.

Kids remember these transgressions in their Care-Friends for a long time. Kathryn was still bringing up that episode years later, in a nice way, when she would be razzing me or kidding with me about not being perfect. I would laugh and razz right back about something she did, of course, but the point was that SHE REMEMBERED. But she remembered it "in a nice way" because I said I was sorry and I didn't do it again. She had good feelings about how I handled it and we kept our trust and love intact.

My dad never said he was sorry. I still remember that to this day. My mom would apologize, and I still remember THAT to this day. My love is stronger for the one who says they're sorry.

On the opposite side, it's vital that we NOT use the word "sorry" when we're right or when we are being the Oak Tree and properly using our Leverage – when our child is going through a tough Lightning Moment and we have our foot down. We feel for them, of course, but we shouldn't say something like, "I'm sorry, but I just can't let you borrow the car. You've been too reckless with it. Maybe in a week or so, if I feel like you'll treat it right."

You are not REALLY sorry in that moment. You may feel bad that your son or daughter won't be able to join their friends by using your car, but you're also upset that they haven't honored your property, so you had to pull out your property Leverage to get their attention – to focus on your rights.

Women are usually the ones who use the "I'm sorry" phrase when they are having to be tough about something. But, unfortunately, what it conveys to the other person, including children, is that you are being weak in that moment – that you are focused right THEN on how bad you feel – instead of on what THEY are doing. THAT is not an Oak Tree, and THAT will be taken advantage of by children looking for a Path of Least Resistance through YOU. It's a small thing, but it's a BIG thing.

Moreover, saying "I'm sorry" when you're really not is not totally honest. Everything we say around everyone should be the exact truth – and children are ALWAYS watching for the exact truth. If they see contradictions, and they are not yet fully rational and in control, they will exploit your "I'm sorry". If they are in rational control, they'll wonder why you're being weak. Save your "sorry" for when you're truly sorry.

Stay strong!

"Sharing" Seems to Be the Hottest Word

One Internet blogger-mom who is against forcing kids to share had this to say about sharing: "Sharing is weird. As adults, do we share our cars? Our ottomans? Our husbands? Last I checked, I wasn't a sister-wife!"

Ha!

The parents' property is not the children's property, and the children's property is not the parents' property. Kids can't tell us what to do with our cars and ottomans, and we can't tell them what to do with their cars and toys.

Many parents think that sharing is a sign of goodness. THIS is the real problem. Voluntary sharing is a sign of affection or benevolence towards others. Sharing is only self-full when a person WANTS to share with someone else. It doesn't mean we're being GOOD in that moment. It just means we are FEELING good about that person and want to give them something.

Someone telling us to surrender our car to a neighbor does not make us a good person, no matter how badly the neighbor needs it, and a parent telling their child to surrender their toy to a neighbor's child does not make the child good. It actually has just the opposite effect on kids and us. It makes us resentful.

It isn't "selfish" to not what to share with strangers or someone we don't have good feelings for – or even if we're just not in a mood to share our things right now. Children don't need to be "taught" how to share. When they are free to run their own lives and know that they own all their own stuff, they share quite freely, just like adults, with those they like – and they enjoy it as much as us adults do when we share our things with those whom we like.

And, of course, the most important point is that our kids have the right to own their own property and determine what to do with it, just as we do. Any parent who takes their kids' property from them as punishment or forces their kids to surrender their property to others is telling the kids: "Your property is not really your property. It is mine to do with as I please – when I please."

Talk about wrecking a Care-Friend relationship!

Trust flies right out the window in such circumstances – and makes it impossible for our kids to listen to us when we are Happy Oak Trees. In fact, we can't really be Happy Oak Trees if we are taking things from our kids or forcing them to give their things to those we choose to be the recipients.

If other parents bring their children to our free houses and expect our children or their children to share, the best thing to do is calmly explain upfront about the right to ownership in our homes – and that we also don't accept items that others have been forced to surrender to us.

This creates some interesting conversations with some parents, who are used to forcing their kids to do things. They may even ask you (in a concerned voice) if you're worried your child will be "selfish". My response was usually something like, "Oh, she is selfish in a good way. She shares with those she likes – so you can always tell whom she likes. Just watch! (with smile)

The famous American writer Ayn Rand, whom I mentioned earlier on "rights", said that all good people are selfish. She meant the good selfish. I prefer the term "self-full", but her point was that good people (self-full people) are the ones who have goals in their life, work hard to attain them, and don't walk over others to get them. Self-full people enjoy their lives and enjoy sharing their life and things with those they respect and like.

(By the way, I agree with Ms. Rand when she says that everyone, including parents, must first make themselves happy before they can help make others happy – even their kids. Perhaps that's for another book.)

Owning our own things is also important for achieving our goals in life. We can't attain our goals if others can take our stuff willy-nilly. We need our property to make things, to go places, to enjoy things. If a neighbor could come take our car or blender or cooking utensils whenever she liked, how would we cook dinner? How would we feel if at any moment we could be forced to share anything, so that our goals in life were always precarious? How could we be self-fulfilled, self-full, without ownership of our property?

Kids feel this way, too. They are seeking their own happiness by going down their Paths of Least Resistance toward their cherished goals. How can they be happy if at any moment, a parent can snatch their phone or their car or their toy or their iPad or their Crayons?

Forced sharing creates great anxiety and anger – especially in kids, because not only do they not have the ability to go out and work and replace the things that got forcefully taken from them, but they also don't have recognized rights in our society to be able to say "No" to those forcing them to "share" their stuff. They are in a serious, anxious pickle if their rights aren't honored by us.

It's time to honor our children's rights to their property and put an end to do-gooder, coercive sharing.

The "Incredulables"

When a bad Path by anyone around us is so bad that humor wouldn't even work, I find incredulity (disbelief) to be the best thing to express.

If an adult friend purposely farts loudly while several of us are talking in the living room, only incredulity (perhaps with a raised eyebrow) works – and possibly follow-up with sarcasm such as "Are you paralyzed, John. Do your legs not work well enough for you to leave the room when you want to be disgusting?"

We are incredulous. So let's express it. And let's express it with our kids when they do something outrageous. In fact, let's call ourselves **The Incredulables**. (I watched The Incredibles with my daughter at least five times, and I think life is a little bit like being a superhero, so hey, us parents are **The Incredulables**!)

Incredulity gets people's attention. They see that you are in disbelief at their actions. They look at your incredulous face and they tap into that disbelief, and it makes them think to themselves "What the heck am I doing to cause THAT face?" It works 20 times better than anger. It's off-the-charts terrific.

It works great by just saying the person's name with your eyebrows raised up in wonderment or shaking your head in disbelief or having a smirk or tilting your head or adding a quip to the whole shebang. Adults do this with each other, especially when one of us makes a remark that is just plain crazy or even stupid. It works equally well with children on bad Paths. I probably had 50 Incredulable moments with Kathryn.

The biggest Incredulable moment was when she was about 8. There was a strange middle-aged man cruising our neighborhood occasionally in a beat-up car. I and my neighbor friends confronted the guy in the street on the fourth day it happened, and it turned out he was a harmless friend of someone down the street and he just liked to drive REAL slow and look at the flowers in people's yards. Nice man, really.

But before we were sure about that, I told Kathryn about the man and she agreed it would be best for her to not go in the front yard after dark until I got it resolved about the man. She had almost always been very rational about danger and was very self-full, but this time she went to the front yard after dark the VERY day that I recommended she shouldn't – and she had agreed.

When I heard her in front with one of her best friends in the pitch-black night, I could hardly believe my ears. I turned on the front porch light and walked out the front door. She stopped playing and looked at me. With a look of utter incredulity on my face, I said, "Kathryn, please tell me that that is not you I see, but instead an imposter who has a mask that looks exactly like you, since I just said a little while ago that there is a strange man cruising our neighborhood and it might not be safe for kids to be out after dark without an adult and you said you agreed. Has my imagination gotten the best of me?!"

She said simply, "It's me." (One of those moments when a straight, innocent reply from a child makes you want to smile.) Because the concern for her safety in this matter had been so overwhelming for me, I was quite emotional, so this was one of the few moments in raising her that I had to remind myself that she has full rights to run her own life. I wanted to get mad at her for being so reckless about her safety, but, after all, it IS her life. This was a Lightning Moment. I reminded myself that I'm not her authority. I am her Care-Friend caretaker. What do I do?

So I said, "Alright, looks like you don't trust my judgment or you didn't really agree with me or you agreed and then decided you didn't. So instead of going back inside to chat with everybody, I'm going to sit here on the front porch until y'all decide to go back inside. I want you to be safe."

She said, "I'm real sorry. I'm real real sorry. I didn't think it would be dangerous. You don't have to stay out here with me ..."

I interrupted, "Oh, I DO have to stay out here with you because ..."

She interrupted, "No, I mean you don't have to stay out here with us because we're coming back in and we aren't coming back out, and I don't want you to have to stay out here."

My heart melted at her thoughtfulness. I said, "OK, sweetie, I appreciate it. But from now on, if you're going to do something that might be dangerous, please come get me first so I can be there – no matter WHAT I'm doing. I'd rather be with you to be sure you're safe than to be talking with ANYBODY!"

She said, "I will, but I don't think it was dangerous." We hugged. Then she said again, "But I really didn't think it was dangerous." I told her, "I understand. Do you mind if we talk more about it later, so we can figure it all out?" She nodded.

In the above scenario, the Leverage I used to ensure safety and still honor her rights was Kathryn's love for me and her caring for my time and fun. By calmly letting her see that her decision to get in harm's way was now costing me my time with my friends, I put the ball back in her court and made it tough for her to carry on with her actions while she knew I'd be sitting there all alone.

I wasn't sacrificing myself in that situation because I truly did want to be there to ensure her safety. I wasn't holding a grudge, because it was truly what I wanted to do, under the circumstances. She knew that and felt the love, but now every moment of her time would be at my expense, and that was too much for her, so she went inside.

This kind of "love" Leverage has to be built up between Care-Friend and child. They know you love them deeply and are always honoring their rights. So they truly don't want to cause you harm or inconvenience.

None of us is perfect, and kids aren't either, of course. But raising a child free usually keeps them from taking too large of a risk because they have a strong sense of themselves and their surroundings and aren't rebelling. They are "present".

When I talked to Kathryn later, she said she didn't think she was taking a risk. I asked her why she went to the front yard after agreeing with me. She said that she and her friend had discussed it and felt like they could run inside fast if the man's car came up the street. When I told her he could park down the street and sneak up on them in the dark, she got frightened and couldn't believe she hadn't thought of that.

Both of us learned something from this episode. She learned that danger wasn't always obvious and that you had to think it through well. And I learned that when I explained danger or anything else, I needed to cover all of the facts and all of my thoughts, so that I would be utterly convincing in my warnings. Our children's incredible brains have to be fully convinced of something, just like us adults when someone is trying to convince us. She never did that or anything so dangerous again.

Getting back to being the Incredulable in that situation, my showing of my incredulity got her to be introspective immediately on what was going on. Her life is her own and she wasn't harming someone else, so I didn't show anger. If I'd gone outside yelling, she would've gotten defensive, and there would've been no good conversation between us. If I would've yelled, it would have implicitly told her that I was her boss

– when I'm not. (When she was four, I started telling her that she was the boss of herself and I was the boss of myself. We would get into fun "boss" games, laughing and saying things like, "Oh NO, I'm the boss of YOU!")

While I was being the Incredulable on the front porch, I was also going back over the FACTS (kids love facts), allowing her to absorb both my real emotions and the real facts in real-time. Incredulity and good-hearted humor/sarcasm are, I think, the twin sisters of effective handling of life and, sometimes, people, including kids.

A sense of humor and good-natured sarcasm and wit are a necessity, I think, in all of us – and they certainly make raising children a TON more fun and effective. Us Incredulables MUST have our sense of humor in many Lightning Moments! It's so much more respectful than an authoritarian "No!" or "Don't".

Ages 4 to 7 – The Pirate Lets Out the Sails

Last month, as I came down my street from a run in my neighborhood, I heard an elderly neighbor's adult daughter yelling at her three daughters (between ages 4 and 7). She told them they must come out from behind the shed in the back yard so the mother could "see" them. She demanded it. They obeyed reluctantly.

I admit that I stopped for a moment to stretch my legs, so I could eavesdrop. I'm a bit of a snoop. I was horrified by this woman's tone and what she said to the girls.

There was no immediate danger. The shed area was clean. And even if there had been danger, it would've been far more efficient and safe for the children if the mom had run there to get them out of harm's way – not to mention far more respectful.

As the girls walked out slumped over and upset, the mom evidently felt she needed to give an explanation for her oppressive behavior, so she said sternly, "I can't SEE you behind the shed! I need to SEE you!" The mom then walked off and could no longer SEE the children. Hmm.

This kind of helicopter parenting isn't about safety (seeing the children). It is about control, mistrust, and contempt for fun-loving pirates.

The three cute girls began frolicking and playing again, but occasionally they would look up warily to see if the mom was present. They have already become second-handed (worrying about what others think of what they might say) and "careful" and obedient – perhaps already looking for ways around their controlling mom.

The "X" Factor

The mother had just put a giant "X" on their freedom and carefree play. She'd become the "X" Factor for her children's meaningfulness. She went from Care-Friend to "X" Factor, placing another barrier between her and her daughters' love and trust, reducing the chance of a long-term friendship and increasing the chances of rebellion and exasperation. She, unfortunately, will have rebellious teenage girls – and she'll blame it either on human nature or on the girls or on friends who are "bad influences" – but not on herself.

If the mother had been a true Care-Friend mom who might've been worried about snakes or something else, she would've joined the girls for safety or already told the girls about the potential for danger in that area, and they may have avoided it. Or if it had just come to the mom's mind about the danger, she could've walked briskly to the back of the shed and said, "Hey y'all, I just started thinking about this area back here, and I don't know if there might be some animals like snakes here that we might have to be careful of. What do you think?"

Respect. Thoughtfulness. Trust. Rights. Meaning. Communication. Fun. Self-fullness.

A Care-Friend mom doesn't say DO something or DON'T do something. She doesn't put an "X" on freedom of choice. She simply states the facts, fully respecting kids' rights. If the girls didn't want to leave after hearing of potential snakes (heck, they might get excited, like my daughter does), the Care-Friend can then make a decision to stay and protect or decide that the threat is overblown and walk away, leaving the girls to their pirate adventure of learning and play.

A Care-Friend mom actually joins the adventure, if she's in the mood!

A Care-Friend, like all good friends, devotes more TIME and thoughtfulness to kids. The neighbor's adult daughter didn't care to spend time with her girls – and it is not "caring" to shout AT children to show that you care about their safety.

What this mom doesn't understand is that if you take more time to get involved and communicate with the kids at this age, they become much more confident and independent, building their lives to have meaning and never thinking of rebellion.

Pirate Born and Pirate Bred

Between the ages of 4 and 7, children explode creatively in all directions. They've learned a bit about who they are. They are getting control of their minds and seeing what that magnificent 3 pounds can do. They are confidently messing with everything around them to see what it is and what it can do and whether it's a Path they wish to explore more deeply. They are getting a clearer idea about what they want. They are enormous bundles of energy finding some treasure on virtually every new island they explore.

If we were the good Watchmen in their first year and honored their rights since then and were the Happy Oak Tree to keep their Paths always from swerving into others' rights, then this four year explosive period of their lives will be a true Pirate Adventure of incredible learning and exploration.

You will rarely have to use Leverage because your communication and involvement in their lives has been off-the-charts wonderful. They've seen your Oak Tree at least a dozen times and possible three dozen times, so they KNOW you will stand by your rights, others' rights and THEIR rights. They trust your judgment. They will challenge you with their new minds because that's what new minds do – but they don't mean the challenge to be insulting. They are simply testing everything around them, including YOU. It's natural. It's good. It's fun. It keeps you on your toes.

When you do have to use Leverage when they are on a bad Path, it is usually brief, because they know you won't bend and that you are probably right.

But sometimes … sometimes bad Paths happen …

Matt's Mess in the Livingroom

For example, let's say that 6-year-old Matt keeps leaving his toys and clothes in the livingroom instead of cleaning up when he's done in the livingroom. You reminded him once nicely, and the second time you reminded him, you pulled out your Incredulable with a pleasantly raised eyebrow and said, "Matt, what, pray tell, might this mess be that I'm looking at AGAIN?" He laughs and cleans up. As he cleans up, you say in an easy but firm voice, "Matt, remember, big guy, that I'm not a butler or maid, right? We all clean up after ourselves so that others don't have to walk around it and look at it. I clean my stuff and you clean your stuff, right? "Yes." ... "Excellent."

I've usually found it best in this second occurrence to not give warnings about the "next time it happens". That, I think, is a bit condescending, assuming that there WILL be a next time. The best thing to do is simply think to yourself, "If this happens again, he's obviously not taking responsibility seriously, so it'll be time for the Oak Tree and Leverage." Also, warnings tend to get children doing things because of "warnings" instead of something just being the right thing to do.

So, a few days later, the Mess From Hell happens again. The bad Path of Least Resistance STRIKES AGAIN. He's wanting to do go down other Paths and breezily forgets to clean because it interferes (too much resistance) with the other Paths. Time for the Oak Tree and Leverage, because he's obviously not finding it important enough to make a mental note to handle his own stuff. Got to draw his attention to the importance of your rights and the fact that relationships take work, mental notes, and mutual recognition.

"Hey Matt. Will you please come here?" When he arrives, stand confidently and silently for a second (not angrily) looking at his mess, so that he can see you. "Here's your mess again, big guy. Yep, I think I'm done with this." He may try to interrupt with an apology or start cleaning immediately, but it's too late. "I appreciate you trying to explain and to clean up now, but this is the third time in six days that you made a mess and then just walked away without cleaning up." (Facts, facts, facts. Kids GET facts. When you say it with those facts, he KNOWS you're right. No getting around it.) "I'm feeling like you're not respecting me and my livingroom."

A kid who's been raised free will honestly feel bad at this point and try to apologize again, but it's too late for that. If you buckle after he's done it three times, he'll continue to do it. Even a free-raised child will keep taking Paths of Least Resistance against you if you buckle, because they haven't yet got the full ability to stay rational and hold onto good principles – which are simply overwhelmed by their immediate emotional desire to have fun down another path.

Using Leverage to Get Matt On A Good Path

Now you bring in your Leverage and take away something of yours for a bit that he really needs, so that he GETS the mutuality of relationships and the importance of honoring your rights, like you do his. Be sure to remain the unflappable Oak Tree as you say the following:

"Matt, I'm not feeling like you are taking me and my clean livingroom very seriously because you keep messing it up and not cleaning, so I'm not feeling like I want to make you any chocolate-chip cookies that I was planning on cooking tonight. I have to feel like you are taking care of me like I take care of you."

It is never easy to have to use Leverage, but be sure to say it thoughtfully and matter-of-factly and do NOT say you are "sorry" for what you have to do at ANY time, as I discussed before. You are right. You have to show that you are right. He has to feel the full impact of his actions, and YOU are the loving deliverer of reality in this Lightning Moment. If you don't do it now, other people who don't care about him in his life will use harsher methods to get him to avoid bad Paths.

Stay strong and stay nearby, because he's going to be upset and probably want to talk about your decision on the cookies, which is always good. Staying nearby means you understand he's upset and needs to talk and that you love and care for him in these difficult moments.

Matt may say he's cleaning up his mess now and ask when you will make the cookies (kids are ALWAYS on a Path). This is a natural question. Turn it around on him with an easy question. "When are you going to start cleaning up your messes all the time, darling?" He'll most likely tell you that starting now, he will always clean his messes. But you have proof that that isn't the case and, as they say, actions speak louder than words – and you HAVE to see consistent actions. Words are an easy Path for children who haven't yet learned to abide by principles. It takes kids a while to get principles (like "rights"), but they understand good RULES quite quickly.

Right now, frankly, you're just not feeling the love from Matt. You may have even been a little pissed, which I would be, and our upset emotions are valid in these times. Our anger doesn't mean we're out for retribution against our kids on bad Paths, but we do need respect – and WE are the only ones who can ensure we get that respect by being Oak Trees. If you need to, tap into that valid anger to stay calmly firm. You MUST get respect for your rights and have a happy child who always finds good Paths to explore without stepping on others.

So, when Matt tells you that he'll starting cleaning up after himself now, be sure to give him the facts about him saying that twice before and it didn't happen.

At this point, however, you wouldn't want to leave him or any other friend hanging on about when you'll start doing something for them again. Here are the two rules that I almost always went by:

1) Keep using your Leverage for at least a day or two. A day is a short time for us adults but a very long time for younger kids, so this gets your respect point across well. They have to WAIT, and it makes them realize that you are upset and you are serious and you are an Oak Tree who won't live with an unfair situation.
2) You must see several examples of good Paths concerning the bad situation before you'll stop using your Leverage.

With the above two rules in mind, you can say something like this to Matt:

"I'm thinking I might make the cookies tomorrow night if you keep cleaning up your messes, like you say you will. If you do, I'll make the chocolate-chip cookies tomorrow after dinner. Alright?"

A child like Matt who was raised free around an Oak Tree will simply say "alright" at this point, because they've learned that resistance is futile – and because they know you're being fair, and kids really do like for things to be fair (Just listen to them argue over who got the most ice cream! Ha!)

All of that said, if it happens again with Matt, you'll need to make it two days of seeing good Paths before you're ready to release your Leverage. Stick by this!

Fixing Matt the Rebel

For those parents who already have children from 2 years old to 17 years old and are just now incorporating the ideas of this book to honor your children's rights, you will most likely have to deal with a potentially angry and rebellious Matt in the above Lightning Moment, especially once you start using your cookie Leverage.

Though you love your children, they have not seen you consistently honor their rights, and they have not seen you be a Happy Oak Tree to ensure that they honor others' rights while on their Paths. There's been some intermittent anger and rebellion and not listening and not communicating and not caring in the family through the years.

Unfortunately, there is no slow detox for you and the kids. When you start being the Oak Tree, they will not believe it and they WILL rebel and test your resolve. But you KNOW this ahead of time and can polish up that resolve by reminding yourself of how important it all is.

Ironically, younger kids come around to the Oak Tree life much faster than older kids. Perhaps it isn't ironic, really, because the older kids have seen your parenting pattern for many years. But both young and old will get it soon enough. Stay strong and congratulate yourself with a half glass of wine or a few bites of your favorite chocolate after you handle a Lightning Moment well. I sure did, and each time I did a toast to me AND my free child!

Before we begin talking about fixing Matt, there are two vital steps that all parents with rebel kids should do:

1) Tell them that you are about to change the way you parent them and that you will be a Happy Oak Tree who honors their rights all the time, and that will mean they will have to start honoring your rights all the time. Because you've read this far, you know all that of that entails.

2) Apologize for how you haven't honored their rights in the past and been occasionally unfair, and say that you plan to never do those things again. You are dedicated now to always being fair with them and letting them explore their pirate lives as you explore yours.

With a "Matt" who hasn't been raised free, there will probably be several points in the above livingroom mess example at which he will test you. Prep yourself!

When he walks into the livingroom and sees your new Incredulable face and you mention the mess, he may just sit on the couch in an "I don't care" mode or even be brazen and say "So?" or "I don't want to clean it now" or "I was coming back out later to clean it" or "Please clean it for me, mommy!".

All the answers above break the fair rule about cleaning up after oneself, and he knows it, ranging from being a smart-ass to being clever to being whiney. Your thoughts on the answers may range from "Alrighty, game on!" to "Ha, that's a good one!"

Run with those thoughts as the Happy (witty) Oak Tree. Humor is that elixir for handling bad Paths in anyone. You should have confident humor because you know this is going to end your way, no matter what – because you know that at any moment, you'll pop the cork on your Leverage and you WILL get good paths sooner or later. It will always go your way, the right way, if you stay on your Leverage until satisfaction.

Here are some sample witty responses to the above five scenarios of rebel Matt:

1) Your response to the "I don't care" plop on the couch: "I've never seen messes cleaned from that position before. Do you use magic?"
2) Your response to the "So" confrontation: "So is a good word. Great beginning to a sentence. Like, let's see, 'Sooooo, it looks like I won't be cooking your chocolate-chip cookies tonight. Sooooo, how's that sound?"
3) Your answer to the "I don't want to clean it now": "Ha, you didn't want to clean a while ago either. What, are you going to wait till you have a beard?"
4) Your response to "I was coming back later to clean it": "Oh, yes, of course, and I think I'll cook those chocolate-chip cookies later, too. Let's see, how about for your 7th birthday LATER this year?"
5) Your response to "Please clean it for me, mommy": "Well, baby, I will clean that for you if you clean my bathroom and the dishes and the floor and my car. How about that. We have a deal?"

These five responses to Matt are not set in stone, obviously. They're meant to convey a certain tone that is necessary for everyone who is dealing with someone doing something to you that they KNOW they shouldn't be doing. They are being obvious in their actions, so you're being obvious with your sarcasm or humor.

We can't argue with someone knowingly violating our rights. Frankly, we have to have a little fun with them, if we can. If we make the mistake of trying to explain the rule AGAIN to someone who already knows the rule, then THEY secretly win, and they will think less of us – for not knowing what they are doing.

Too many parents, especially women unfortunately, attempt to explain over and over again what the rule is that the child is breaking, when the child knows quite well what the rule is. This is where parental condescension bites parents in the rear, because they think the child is too dumb to understand rules the first time. A good female friend of mine used to "state the obvious" repeatedly, and all she got in return was the same blank look – and bad behavior over and over again. Thank goodness she doesn't do it anymore, and she's got great kids.

If you go right after a bad Path with wit and confidence, you turn the tables on the person, adult or child, who is violating your space, time or property. Your humor and sarcasm can actually be a bit annoying to those who had hoped to get something over on you. When they see your confidence, they know your resolution, and they know they will have to come around to what is fair – eventually.

In each of the five examples, Matt clearly knows what he's doing. He knows the fair rules of cleanup, so each of his comments is a "play" for weakness, for a bad Path of Least Resistance – to get what he wants the fastest and easiest way, via parental weakness. Each comment boils down to a challenge of the parent's fortitude. They've put the ball in your court to see what you'll do with it. An Oak Tree return puts the ball back in their court to serve up a good Path.

Before I continue, I need to stress that children don't feel good about themselves when they take bad paths. They may seem to do it very quickly and easily, but it makes them anxious, because they know it isn't fair and that they are manipulating another person to get something they know they shouldn't get. They don't even know they are WANTING you to be an Oak Tree who stops them from taking the bad Path that runs over others. They haven't learned to be their own Oak Tree yet.

Children who aren't around Oak Tree Care-Friends make a habit of taking bad Paths and skirting responsibility. We unfortunately see these kinds of children almost every day in our lives.

The Oak Tree and Matt

Whichever way the scenario with Matt begins to play out and starts playing out, there are two things you simply can't do as an Oak Tree:

1) **Don't clean up his mess**, even if it means it stays there for a week in a Leverage showdown worthy of a Western movie. If you want your lovely child to be a permanent friend who respects himself, you and others, you cannot cow to him in Lightning Moments. Every time you walk by the mess, think of it as a temporary necessity that will be fixed eventually.

2) **Don't be a nag.** Nagging tells others that we don't respect their ability to get things done by themselves. "Reminding" someone about things regularly is also a form of nagging. If we are reminding someone about things constantly, we don't think they care enough to get it done themselves. As Dr. Gray said in a quote earlier in this book, this kind of parental behavior ends up creating the behavior it wishes to avoid, by EXPECTING the child to never care.

Matt may decide he wants a showdown on the mess. Maybe he senses that you are changing (for the good) and he's not liking the new Oak Tree who doesn't bend on bad Paths. Maybe he thinks that if he doesn't stop your firmness right now, he'll never have his old Paths of Least Resistance that run right through you.

If that's the case, dig your heels in and go about enjoying yourself in your life – and use even more Leverages, if necessary. You may need to tell him that you're not feeling like taking him to the ice cream shop with the other kids. That is perfectly legit, since he's trying to run over you. Why WOULD you feel like taking him?

You may decide not to let him eat the spaghetti you've just cooked for the rest of the family. This may seem harsh, but HE is being harsh. His CLOTHES are still on the livingroom floor, aren't they?! Tell him he is welcome to make himself some cereal and eat it next to you all while the rest of you have spaghetti. You obviously don't want your lovely son to be an outcast, but you certainly don't want to be doing something for somebody who is showing no intention of respecting your rights.

Sooner or later (usually sooner), Matt GETS the Oak Tree thing. And, frankly, the spaghetti episode, or something like it, may be the turning point. Sooner or later, he realizes how much he relies on you and how MANY things you do for him, and that living without your love or property or caretaking or money is simply not acceptable to him anymore.

Once he sees that you truly MEAN what you say and you act on it with complete happiness and confidence, he's done. But he DOES have to see that, and you have to feel like you are truly doing the right thing. THAT is one of the big things this book is about. You ARE doing the right thing – everybody is honoring everyone else's rights.

Planes, Trains, Dolls, Clothes, Ice Cream and Automobiles

Two weeks ago, my daughter and I and some of her friends and a good friend of mine were sitting outside one of our favorite ice cream shops on a patio, sweetening our palates. A nice-looking couple in their early 30s came on the patio with their 1-year-old boy and five-year-old girl.

My friend and I engaged the parents in conversation as all the kids played around and ate their ice cream. The conversation was smooth and pleasant. The mom was pleasant with her baby boy, wiping his mouth and watching over him. The girl was a little shy and cautious but having fun with our older kids.

I had to run to my car briefly, and soon after that my daughter and my friend came up to me and told me that the following happened while I was gone.

The couple decided suddenly to leave, and they gave their little girl no warning. (Us adults don't do that to our friends, and yet parents do this to their children all the time: no warning, as if they aren't people at all.) The girl didn't want to go, but the mom put on her stern voice and said they had to go right now. Then the mom took it one step further.

She told the little girl that she had to carry her little brother's shoes. The girl said no and that the shoes smelled and she shouldn't have to carry them. That's when the mom pulled out the punitive threat that is so characteristic of many parents throughout history.

"If you don't carry his shoes, we will NEVER bring you back here to eat ice cream!"

My friend and my daughter said they were furious to hear this and that their hearts broke for the little girl as they watched her stricken face.

She picked up the shoes delicately and remained quietly obedient, as if completing a task of unimaginable disgust.

This little girl did not give birth to her brother. She wasn't the parent. She did not decide to have a child, as her parents did. The parents took on the responsibility for having another child, and then they threaten their first child with retribution if she doesn't take care of the second child when they demand it.

My daughter, whose rights have been honored since birth, was incensed. Kathryn and I discussed this, as we've discussed almost everything in our lives together since she was 3. She judges adults as easily as kids, and her assessment of the parents at the ice cream shop was not pleasant, understandably.

The little girl at the ice-cream shop had a right to run her own life in what could've been a lovely moment of her life – as my daughter and my friend's children got to experience. But her beautiful moment collapsed around her. She may now actually associate bad feelings with the ice cream shop. This is, almost certainly, not the first time the X Factor has happened to the little, sweet pirate.

We all know that these parents wouldn't dare treat friends that way, making such demands, and yet someone smaller and more fragile and dearer to them receives this treatment without the parents' giving it a second thought.

Had the parents raised their daughter to be free, they would've simply said "would you mind?" when asking her to carry the shoes. And the free daughter would've known it was her decision – and probably would've made a funny remark about the smelly shoes and then probably would've picked them up in a funny manner, with everyone around her laughing, including my daughter and friend.

And if she'd said "no thanks", Oak Tree parents wouldn't have given it a second thought, because it is her life and THEIR son. They would WANT her to do only what she wanted to do in the moment, just like them.

This ice cream example extends to all of our parenting, if we are forcing our kids to do something that we wouldn't force an adult friend to do. Our friends have their lives to live meaningfully, and our kids have the same lives and the same rights. Our priorities are not necessarily their priorities. Their priorities in the moment may be planes or dolls or cars or gaming or clothing or trains or chilling out or phones or architecture or conversation or cooking or cleaning or ice cream. If our priority in the moment is to have our 1-year-old's shoes picked up, then WE can do it ourselves or ask someone else to help us with that priority. That's it! Our kids are not our butlers or maids or nannies.

Many parents force their older kids to take care of the parents' younger children. This thought, frankly, should never enter a good parent's mind, except when asking politely for help. An older child should be able to get up in the morning with zero dread of being forced to do anything, including being a nanny. They should hear that snare shot and pursue their own meaning every minute of every day.

Ages 8 to 12 – The Wonder Years

The reason I spent so much time on 6-year-old Matt is to show a basic paradigm of how us Oak Trees handle our Leverage in all Lightning Moments. The only thing that really changes much from Matt's example is the age of the child. When their age changes, so does the context of our situation with them. We can expect more from older kids and talk to them a little differently – but the Leverage doesn't change. We still use a little or lot of Leverage to ensure that a bad Path turns good, and all rights are honored.

If we've been Happy Oak Trees honoring our kids' rights and not controlling them through the age of 7, then once they turn 8, they truly GET rules and rights and responsibility. They know they are free – and they must honor others' freedom.

This doesn't mean they're perfect, of course. They still mess up occasionally, but the mess-up is brief, and communication by you is usually enough to bring them to a good Path. Usually, by the age of 12, there are no more mess-ups with free kids than there are with our adult friends. Until then, though, they slide a bit on some things.

For example, kids between 8 and 12 have gotten so awesome handling things and finding meaning in their lives that they get caught up in those things and forget chores. They haven't gotten perfect yet at putting a "standing order" in their head that they have to occasionally drop the fascinating thing they're doing so that they can take out the trash or do the dishes or clean the cat boxes or mow the yard or mop the floor or clean the bathrooms or chop up the veggies for dinner or keep the noise down, etc.

As with our adult friends or spouses, this isn't a problem if it's just a one-time thing, but if it becomes routine or even intermittent, then they are expecting someone else (us) to take care of those things, by default. And "default" means not respecting other parties. Default means they don't wish to put forth the mental energy to keep their side of the bargain. Default means their Path of Least Resistance is running over us and possibly others.

A default bad Path means we have a Lightning Moment, to ensure that we don't have to do their work or that we don't fall into the trap of becoming nags to get them to do what they're supposed to do anyway. They're capable of keeping their Paths good and honoring us; they're just not making the effort to do it.

One quick comment on chores. Because we do so much for our children and because they also makes messes, dividing up work around the common-area part of the house is totally fair – a necessity. You're doing the cooking, so why shouldn't they do the dishes? They're sharing OUR bathroom, so why shouldn't they clean it sometimes. They're sharing OUR livingroom, so why shouldn't they dust or vacuum occasionally. They use OUR yard to play in, so why shouldn't they do some of the work there as well?

The word "chores" has long had a bad connotation, but maybe it shouldn't. We love a clean bathroom, a clean floor, clean dishes, a trimmed yard. We love the end product of doing our chores. Free kids also love to take responsibility for their surroundings and enjoy things to be crystal clean. In fact, they like to walk up to their Care-Friends and say, "Hey, come look at the sink. I made it super shiny."

Staying the Oak Tree with kids helps them to eventually enjoy the responsibility and enjoy the cleanliness. And, of course, being an Oak Tree means that YOU take the responsibility for your chores, and you are a terrific example for your lovely children.

And since our kids SHOULD be doing these chores, we shouldn't be offering them "allowances" or "rewards" for work that is expected and fair. We shouldn't be trying to bribe people, including children, to do the things they should already be doing. And, frankly, their "allowance" is everything we do for them, and they should know that. If we ask them to do extra work, and they agree, then yes, of course, giving them money for that is terrific.

The expectation of chores is the expectation of fairness.

E-X-P-E-C-T and R-E-S-P-E-C-T

Which brings me to a vital aspect of being the Happy Oak Tree all the time.

Expectations.

We should EXPECT everyone around us, including our kids, to RESPECT our rights and others' rights always. We want our respect and we deserve it. A child continually messing up on doing chores means we're not getting the respect for our time and space that we deserve. We should expect that time and space to be respected.

And we MUST act on that expectation of respect. We must act in those Lightning Moments – even if it's been six months since they had a bad Path and Lightning Moment – or we will lose respect for ourselves and from those we love. Even if our child is simply awesome almost all the time, we must act. We should be benevolent but firm Watchmen our entire lives with everyone. And, frankly, in life, when it comes to our rights or nearly anything else, "almost" just doesn't cut it.

When we get up in the morning, we should be drinking our coffee or tea with the knowledge that we handled the previous day's Lightning Moment well and that our kids are awesome because of it, and our day's beginning is the "snare shot" – and so is our child's!

Stu's Chores

So, let's say your 10-year-old has "forgotten" chores twice in the last week. The first time, you just said, "Hey, Stu, you forgot to take the trash to the street." No problem. He takes care of it and apologizes.

The second time, you say with a slight casual Oak Tree smirk, "Hey, Stu, dishes still in the sink and they aren't washing themselves. You forgot the trash the other day, and now the dishes, but you didn't forget to call your friends and talk for three hours."

He says apologetically, "Oh, yeah, I totally blanked. I'll do that now."

That's a good response, but … a pattern is a pattern, and you're getting taken advantage of. You ask him to talk after he finishes the dishes. He says of course. He knows what's up – he's been through the Happy Oak Tree before. The thing to discover in the talk is whether you think the forgetfulness is willful or absent-mindedness. If it's a willful "whatever" attitude, then you'll use Leverage with him right now. But if he's been a free-raised kid, then it's most likely absent-mindedness.

If you determine it's absent-mindedness, then y'all sit down, he apologizes again and says he'll set a reminder in his phone so he wont' forget again, which is great that he's thinking that far ahead. He seems sincere and very apologetic.

He says again that he just blanked. You think he's sincere about not forgetting anymore, but a shot across the bow is still necessary, so he knows the Oak Tree wants to enjoy her days without having to worry about others stepping on her.

Again, I find that quips are good at this point, such as, "You didn't 'blank' on your four hours of gaming with your friends, but you 'blanked' on your chores, which take only a few minutes? Have I got that right?" (Sarcasm and quips and humor are about seeing the contradictions or irony in something, so they bring home the facts in a whimsical but biting way. It's also good to use other people's words back at them in a clever way.)

I might follow up that quip with something like, "Well, do you think I might 'blank' on taking you to baseball practice tomorrow afternoon? If I'm not feeling the love here, Stu, wouldn't that possibly make me 'blank' in taking care of you?"

He gets it and says, "I understand. I'll set my phone calendar from now on."

You say OK and nod your head with a look of love but also expectation. "OK. Thanks, sweetie. I believe you, and I'm sure you believe me about the baseball practice." He nods his head seriously and knows the Oak Tree is not kidding. All is good.

If he forgets a chore again soon after that, don't even have a discussion. He's 10 years old and is well past the years of not being able to remember promises. Just walk up and say, "Stu, is your calendar broken?" He'll probably figure out right away that he's forgotten the trash or whatever. He might even jump up and say "Damn" and run and take care of the trash.

But it's too late. You HAVE to be the Oak Tree now. If you aren't, he'll never respect you and he won't respect his own commitments. His third lapse proves that the chores are not a priority in his head and that his verbal commitments are not solid commitments, so he'll need your Leverage to see that respect works both ways.

Just say matter-of-factly, "I'm sure you know I won't be taking you to baseball practice on Thursday, like we talked about before." You know how much you love him and how much he loves his practice, but respect for rights and commitments is far more important than his practice right now. There will always be other practices, but there will only be so many Lightning Moments where our children must GET the rights of others – and the fact that what they say must MEAN something.

You can have a long discussion with him, if he wants, at this point, but you cannot take away the Leverage on the practice, no matter how apologetic or upset he may be. You MUST stand as the Oak Tree, no ifs, ands or buts. He must see that you have so much respect for yourself that you won't be walked on.

At this point, he has the right to find another parent to take him to practice, so if he does that, then take away another Leverage. He must FEEL your Leverage. Find something he really needs you for that can't be replaced by someone else, whether it's your cooking or new baseball equipment or new shoes or your taking him across town for something or the Wi-Fi you pay for that his TV or phone or tablet needs, etc. You can't take away his phone or tablet or TV if they are his property, but you can take away YOUR property, which is the Wi-Fi.

In this case, you might say something sincere like, "I see you got someone else to give you a ride to practice. Good for you. Since that is the case, I'll be taking away my Wi-Fi connection until it seems to me that you're holding up your part of the house bargain on chores. Thanks."

(You are keeping your head about you and sticking to facts. We don't have to be the lovely but neurotic Lorelai Gilmore when putting our foot down with loved ones. She once said, "I'm afraid that once your heart's involved, it all comes out in 'moron'"! Ha! Funny, but no, it doesn't have to be that way. It CAN'T be that way if we are to be the Oak Tree.)

If Stu goes to a neighbor's house to play his games after you shut down his Wi-Fi access, then use another Leverage that he needs from you. Continue upping the Leverage count, frankly, until his life becomes so complex and difficult that he GETS the point. And remind yourself that all you are doing is taking away YOUR stuff, not his stuff. You're putting rules on the use of your time, property, money, love and communication. That is your right.

And at no point should you be upset that he's going around you to try to keep his Path of Least Resistance. After all, it's his right, but you know that his Path of Least Resistance has gotten a heck of a lot MORE resistant since you're cutting your things out – and eventually he'll get your Oak Tree and realize what is right. He will cut his losses if you hold true to what is right, and you do it with comfortable ease and firmness.

In the above "Stu" example, a child who has been raised free will most likely not do it the third or fourth time, though it's possible they will, but they will GET your Oak Tree very quickly and correct their "Chore Challenge".

But with a 10-year-old who has not been raised to have their meaningful good Path honored all the time and not experienced the Oak Tree, you may have to use as many as five Leverages steadfastly over a period of a week or two to get them to understand your firmness and what is right. Dig your heels in and enjoy your life in the meantime. The problem they are having and the hurt they feel has been brought on by them. And the "problem" is actually their not honoring your rights. The problem is NOT you.

After Stu gets the chores down well and there is perfect harmony again in the home, reward yourself. You deserve it. But be sure to NOT reward Stu or connect what he's done well to any kind of reward. He is simply doing what he's supposed to do, like any good friend should do. We don't reward people for finally treating us right. We EXPECT them to treat us right. Sure, there are good feelings all around now. That's great. So simply enjoy your well-earned Oak Tree love and harmony.

Ages 13 to 17 – The Grown-Up Years

If you've been the Oak Tree Care Friend for the entire life of your child-friend, then these are truly the years of full friendship and respect, with virtually no issues arising at all, outside of the occasional forgetfulness that all friendships incur occasionally – such as a one-time forgotten chore or leaving things lying around or a too-loud party at the house or being late for an appointment or a call late at night on a phone that's not muted or an accidentally broken phone face or no gas left in the car after being used, etc.

Even though teens have tons of new hormones jetting through their system and can be highly emotional at times, if your relationship through the years has been solid, those emotions don't lead to bad Paths. There should be very few Lightning Moments. That may seem impossible to believe, but it's true. They're your friends now! You've built such an incredible foundation of trust and communication and cooperation and love that it really doesn't even occur to your teen (even when they are emotional) that they would walk on you. They love you with all their heart.

I found that that trusting friendship meant that my daughter even called me by my first name occasionally when we were talking, which surprised me at first (a lot!), but when I started thinking about it, it made sense. She and I both saw us as equals, so when we were having conversations, I didn't see her as "child" and she didn't see me as "parent". I'm beginning to think that this is one of the true indicators of equality in the household: a first-name basis by the child occasionally. I've seen it start as early as 8 or 9 years of age. A parent should be proud if this occurs (after you get over the shock!).

I could get into a lot of examples of what teens go through at this age and how you handle your Oak Tree Leverage in Lightning Moments, but I'll just have one more example: of a 15-year-old who brings someone you don't like to your house. The examples previously in the book about Matt and Stu, especially, are the paradigms for you in being the Oak Tree with your older kids, who've reached a level of maturity in which they can understand your use of Leverage quite well.

Use and stick by one or more Leverages to turn the bad Path into a good Path – and don't surrender EVER. Teens who weren't raised free may have the willpower to test you for weeks or months. Be ready for this and use your Five Leverages matter-of-factly and with strength, and you WILL get a good Path eventually.

As with younger children, we don't want to pretend that we are running our teens' lives. It's their life and their meaning, after all. The unfortunate tendency of many parents of teens is to EXPECT bad Paths and to clamp down even harder with false rules, instead of doing quite the opposite – letting them be entirely free to run down their pirate Paths, as long as they don't run over others.

Cara's Friend Ryan

If we adults don't like another adult – whether it's a former friend or acquaintance or family member or whomever – we no longer invite them to our house or let them come to our house. Frankly, we don't want them around, and we own our house, so we use our house as Leverage to ensure that we don't have to put up with that person in our own territory. That's our right.

The same goes for our children's friends. We're very glad of course that our kids have friends and we might like most of their friends, but if one of their friends is consistently disrespectful to our child or us or others we care about or is just not a good person, then we can pull out our house Leverage to protect our rights and to get the attention of our child, who seems a bit blind about their friend's character.

Let's say that 15-year-old "Cara" keeps bringing 16-year-old "Ryan" to our house, but he occasionally says mean things to her and yells at her, and there's even been a few things missing after he's come over. As a Happy Oak Tree, you've talked matter-of-factly to Cara about what you've seen, as you would your adult friends, but she seems a bit blind in her judgment of Ryan and his disrespect of her and your house. She insists that you're wrong and that he's really a nice guy "deep down".

She's got a right to her friends, just like you and your adults friends do, but they don't have a right to YOUR house if they're on a bad Path. You've got the right to your self-full Path, and there can be no guilt about insisting that you be respected all the time while on your own pirate Path.

Time to pull out your Leverage in a conversation with Cara, after you ask her to chat with you for a few minutes:

"Cara, I know we've talked about Ryan and I know you disagree with me about him, but, darling, anyone who insults my loved ones in my house can't come into my house. Remember, I did that with Uncle Steve, too, when he got kind of nasty with you about your ear-piercings and wouldn't apologize?"

"Mom, are you saying that Ryan is as bad as Uncle Steve, really?"

"Probably not. I don't know Ryan well-enough to say. But that's not my point. It's the same situation where somebody is being nasty in my house and being nasty to you, and you know I don't allow people to be nasty to my family in my home. I don't want him in the driveway or the yard, either. If you still want to meet with him here, he's got to stay on the street to pick you up. If he learns to respect you and will respect my home, please let me know, and I'll welcome him back."

"Alright, I think you're being unfair, but I'll let him know."

The main point of the above Leverage conversation is to protect your self-full values: your daughter and your home. But it's also to politely but firmly be the Oak Tree that gets across your judgment of Ryan, so that Cara has an objective outside opinion of her friend – and she has a role model in you. You are standing your ground and so should she. You've done nothing to punish Cara. You've just said plainly, "I'm taking away my property from this boy, but y'all can obviously enjoy others' property, if they allow you to."

Yes, you've made their relationship more of an inconvenience, but that's the point of Leverage – to use your own things to inconvenience bad Paths enough to get those Paths turned into good Paths, or a least to ensure that your rights are protected, so you can be self-full and happy.

It may seem outrageous for me to say, but I've not seen free-raised kids keep bad friends. They drop them like hot potatoes – or the free kids become Oak Trees and use Leverage themselves to get bad-Path kids to straighten up around them. I've seen this dozens of times. Free kids are way too interested in being self-full and having fun with their lives to put up with anyone who is insulting or mean or unfair. They have high self-esteem and judge fairly but firmly, and they stand by their judgments. And once they get to about age 10 or 11, they judge adults almost as easily as they do the kids around them.

But let's say that Cara is a rebel and just blows off what you said about Ryan staying off your property. She doesn't honor your right to your property and she lets Ryan come on your driveway and yard. She knows what she's doing. YOU know what she's doing – challenging you.

We can't fool ourselves when we are Oak Trees in our lives. We KNOW that Cara KNOWS what she is doing by letting Ryan step foot on your property. She is testing you and, frankly, saying to herself, "OK, now what are you going to do?" She wants to see how much of an Oak Tree you are and she wants to stay on her bad Path of Least Resistance.

It's time to escalate your Leverage to change her bad path. You have a right to put boundaries on people's actions on your property – on anything having to do with your self-full Path to independence and happiness.

You've now got two Leverage routes you can take – the semi-hard one or the very-hard one.

The semi-hard one: You can walk out to Cara and Ryan and say calmly to Cara that because Ryan is back on your property, Cara won't be using your car for a while or using your Wi-Fi. (You must ignore Ryan during this exchange because right now it's just about you and Cara. Even if Ryan speaks up, ignore him. Don't even look at him. He hasn't earned your courtesy. Only people who respect us deserve our attention. And this discussion is only between you and your loved one.)

Then calmly walk back to the house without any discussion – as Cara is probably shaking her head or even cussing at you.

The Oak Tree does not bend when she is right. There can be no give-and-take when one side wishes to TAKE something from you. Ryan has taken respect away from Cara, your loved one. And Cara is not respecting you. If we don't stand up for ourselves and our loved ones, then when DO we stand up in life? Life is no good on our knees. We do not sleep well at night if we've been on our knees during the day. But we sleep like babies if we are Oak Trees and self-full during our daily lives.

A Thousand Points of Lightning

I'll get to the very-hard Leverage route in a moment. But first:

Life is full of Lightning Moments, with our kids, with our families, with our lovers, with our friends, with our co-workers, with casual acquaintances. Being an Oak Tree doesn't end after we handle one Lightning Moment well (though it's always good to have a successful Oak Tree Moment). There are thousands of Lightning Moments in our lives – frankly, because people misbehave and don't honor themselves and therefore don't honor us. (This is one reason why some people, unfortunately, become hermits. They aren't confident enough to handle the Lightning.)

I don't mean this to be depressing. It's just a fact of life, so we must be happily self-full and strong our whole life, every day. That is what the last chapter of this book is about. If we are an Oak Tree when we get up every morning, we don't have to worry about any Lightning Moments that may occur. We don't go through our days with antennae up all the time in prickly anticipation of misbehavior. We just get up every morning happy for a new day, but entirely ready for any person attempting a bad Path right down the middle of us. Then we handle it and move on.

In the semi-hard example with the rebel Cara, she may say, "Well, so what. I've got Ryan to drive me around and I don't need your Wi-Fi" – or something like that.

Hard and Fast

Now it's time for the **very-hard Leverage option**. We must always be prepared to take any Leverage to the max, no matter what it is. With

Cara essentially ignoring you and your rights and not taking your Leverage seriously, it's time to talk with Ryan. You can use sarcasm or just plain straight-talk. Here's the sarcastic approach.

"Ryan, how good are you with talking to the police?"

"What?"

"I'm going to be calling the police in a moment to have you removed from my property, if you don't get off of it right now, and I was wondering if you're a good conversationalist."

Cara will try to interrupt and possibly even call you names at this point. Ignore her. It's not about her anymore. It's about YOU and your rights and Ryan.

If Ryan gets off the property and stays off (which he probably will, because you've become too much resistance on his Path), then you're good at this point. If he doesn't, then call the police immediately and, if necessary, get a restraining order against him. Don't mess around with bad people! They may turn out to be good people one day, hopefully, but that's not your business right now.

The "very-hard-Leverage" option may seem drastic to some of you, and perhaps it is drastic. But we must be prepared to be drastic with those on a bad Path who simply won't get the message when we are NOT being drastic with our semi-hard Leverage. Most people, including rebel kids, don't think you'll do it. Once you show that you will (once or twice or more), they eventually DO believe you – and they respect you.

Your Power Key

If you've got rebel teens, then you'll need to learn how to be the Happy Oak Tree and remain the Oak Tree. Remember that your Leverage is your KEY. It is your power. It is the thing that you have that keeps anyone in your lives from running over you, because now you set the terms. You own YOU! You own your love, your money, your communication, your things, and your space. Use them or lose them!

If this book has convinced you that kids are in fact totally awesome with incredible minds and benign pirate outlooks, and it has convinced you that you are their Care-Friend and their Oak Tree for the beginning of their lives and that you CAN be that Oak Tree, then simply honor their lives as pirate teens, enjoy those lives and keep your Leverage handy for them – or anybody else in your life whose bad Path is heading for you.

You got the POWER!

Chapter Fourteen

Lightning Moments
Here's a Laundry List

As you know, Lightning Moments occur when another person's bad Path runs right over us or our rights, or they are being disrespectful towards us, when we don't deserve it. I've talked some about how the Lightning Moments occur with adults also, so in the list below I'm including some Lightning Moments that occur with kids and adults. In each case you would use as much of your Leverage as was necessary to change their bad Path.

1) Chores not getting done
2) Too much noise
3) Messiness in your space (their room can be as messy as they want it)
4) Hitting another person first (instead of self-defense, which is OK)
5) Talking rudely to you ("You're just a stupid old adult")
6) Expecting you to buy them anything they want
7) Recklessness with others' property (broken things or torn-up things)
8) Recklessness with you (trying to drive drunk with you in the car)
9) Bringing bad people around
10) Using or taking your things without your permission
11) Someone at work gossiping about you
12) Lying
13) Deception
14) Nagging ("You really should go to the family reunion. Don't be mean.")
15) Harassment (someone doing something to you or trying to force you to do something you don't want to do)
16) Repeated broken commitments or promises
17) Being unfair and/or mean towards you
18) Expecting you to do things for them that they should be doing
19) Being unsafe with you or others you care about
20) Not even using the things they beg you to buy for them

We all have to deal with dirty laundry – as the Happy Oak Tree. There are hundreds or thousands of potential Lightning Moments in life that we have to handle as the Oak Tree, and the above list is just some that we all encounter.

I wrote the list above to give even more examples of what kind of Lightning Moments we encounter to provide a better understanding of bad Paths, in case that was not already clear.

Chapter Fifteen

Who's the Boss?

Oh, Please Don't Say "Don't"

If we are in charge of ourselves and confident, we don't tell friends, including our child-friends, "Don't". It would be an incredible insult to tell an adult friend "Do as I say" or "Because I said so" or "Don't talk back to me!" (We'd probably get the look of death and an "Excuse me, what did you just say?!)" In fact, that would NEVER enter our minds. We are not their boss.

So it should not enter our minds with our kids as well. We aren't their boss. We're their equals, their temporary Care-Friends who are their physically-bigger equals in life as we travel together in search of our meanings to our lives as free people.

Here's a list of "Don'ts" that indicate that you are in a state of mind (or starting to be in a state of mind) in which you are feeling like the boss of your kids. If you hear yourself think or say any of these "don'ts", then you should step back and re-evaluate the relationship with your children, adjust your thinking to honor their rights and re-affirm that the relationship is one of equality and friendship – not authority.

1) Don't stay up too late
2) Don't stay out too late
3) Don't talk back to me
4) Don't play too many games
5) Don't leave food on your plate
6) Don't get on the Internet
7) Don't tell me I'm wrong
8) Don't judge
9) Don't look at me that way
10) Don't touch anything at the store
11) Don't walk around bare-footed
12) Don't climb too high
13) Don't ride your bike so fast
14) Don't text while driving and don't drive too fast
15) Don't have sex till you're 18
16) Don't wear those clothes
17) Don't get tattoos or piercings
18) Don't cuss
19) Don't leave the toilet seat up (or down)

20) Don't leave your room a mess

All of the above list of 20 are Paths that all or most children take in their lives to be expedient or to experience things or to find information or to express themselves. When it comes down to it, frankly, these things are none of the business of us parents, outside of making sure a child in a store doesn't break anything.

Even texting while driving can be safe in strict circumstances and, like us adults, teens are smart and can determine their own safety in such circumstances – and even whether they want to break the law, like almost every adult driver breaks the law on speeding and texting, because those laws are often absurd. Also, free-born teens are highly responsible and can determine if or when they wish to have sex that they consider safe and meaningful.

But the main point is not whether a parent would be right about any comment on the above list. The main point is, again, that the child has the right to DO those things when and where they wish to do it, along their pirate Path, as long as they are not interfering with or endangering others. We parents have the right to do all those things, so why wouldn't our children? If we tell them "don't" in the above situations, then we are being condescending, thinking that they not only don't have a right to their life but also that they aren't smart enough to make good decisions – or live with the consequences of their bad decisions.

When children are raised free, they are very self-oriented, in the sense that they have a respect for their "self" and are supremely aware of themselves and what they want and how to be safe, to protect their self-fullness. They don't need, and shouldn't experience, a parent or anyone else presuming that they can't take care of themselves and know what Path they wish to take in the moment.

The use of the word "don't" by parents means the parents DON'T want to explain, don't want to respect someone else's mind and rights, don't want to take the respectful route to get what they think is right by explaining themselves respectfully. It is the boss position: "Stop right now because I, the boss, say so."

But kids and adults are only the bosses of themselves.

As I've talked about before, one of the primary purposes of this book is to change our relationship with our kids from boss to friend, by honoring their right to find their own meaning as intelligent human beings. If, by this point in the book, a parent still feels like they should be the boss, then the last chapter of the book is especially important to read, and hopefully you'll change your mind – for your sake and your children's sake.

Chapter Sixteen

School's Out Forever
Life Is the Ultimate Teacher

My favorite quote on "schooling" has always been and still is by Mark Twain:

"I have never let my schooling interfere with my education."

Ha! The hilarious and inspirational Twain left school after the fifth grade. Life was his teacher, and he learned her well. Twain was the embodiment of the independent American spirit and has been, I think, our greatest writer. William Faulkner called Twain the Father of American Literature.

I agree, and yet Twain was "schooled" for only a few short early years. How could he be so smart?! Perhaps it was BECAUSE Twain was schooled for only a few years, with his spirit remaining thankfully intact, putting little stock in obedience or conformity – using his free will to learn what he wished to learn from life.

Twain's point, which I agree with, is that coercive schooling (forcing kids into schools) actually stunts REAL learning – which comes from pirate adventure and chosen paths of interest in each second of one's life. We only truly learn when we seek information on something we are truly interested in. Formal schooling is almost exclusively about memorizing what someone ELSE is interested in or is told to teach. It is about obedience to others instead of devotion to your inner love of life and your inner Path of discovery.

The famous English philosopher Bertrand Russell was a bit more caustic on formal schooling than Twain. Russell called schooling "one of the chief obstacles to intelligence and freedom of thought."

One of the popular jokes among my friends when I was in school and studying for (and worrying about) yet another test was "Don't worry. You'll forget it all the day after the test." Why remember things you're forced to learn and don't care about and that usually don't have any relevance to what you'll be doing in your life? What a horrendous waste of our most valuable commodity – TIME. School, in fact, teaches kids how to get comfortable with wasting time. It teaches lazy-mindedness.

"The whining schoolboy, with his satchel
And shining morning face, creeping like a snail
Unwillingly to school" – William Shakespeare

But we don't creep like a snail to those things that fascinate us. We run like the wind. And we rarely forget them either. My daughter still remembers she and I chasing early-morning grasshoppers and crickets for her pet lizard when she was barely five. She studied Lizzy's habits every day. And she still gets tears in her eyes, to this day, when she talks about "Lizzy" dying in his aquarium after several months of feasting on hoppers and cricks.

Those many years ago, Kathryn decided that we wouldn't bury Lizzy (much to my chagrin!). She wanted Lizzy to turn into a skeleton and see what Lizzy looked like without skin and muscle. (Her curiosity about such technical things at that early of an age startled me, but I eventually realized that all free young minds are that way.)

She studied Lizzy's skeleton for a few weeks before we buried Lizzy. She remarked on his joints and long toes and head structure and much more before she was finally satisfied. THAT is learning you don't forget. That is NOT schooling. It is following your free will. It is remembered with fondness – not the regret or anger or anxiety of forced schooling.

The famous former educator John Taylor Gatto had this to say about schooling:

"When you take free will out of education, that turns it into schooling." Mark Twain would agree.

We are either free or we are not. Our will is either free to choose or it is set upon by those stronger than us or with more coercive power than us – usually parents and teachers. Education that is not freely chosen is not education at all. Yes, you will learn some of it because you have to or because you're momentarily interested, but your free will didn't choose it at that time and place, so it cannot have the depth of meaning that comes from a freely chosen pirate Path. It is not connected to what YOU want.

Widespread "public schooling" ends up creating a society of adults who've become accustomed to not having complete control over their free will, their choices. It creates a society of obedient, anxious and angry adults – who have grown so accustomed to authority that they don't outwardly question rules or bosses or spouses or family members or politicians or the PC culture or even the police.

"We are shut up in schools, and colleges, and recitation rooms, for ten or fifteen years, and come out at last with a bag of wind, a memory of words, and do not know a thing." – Ralph Waldo Emerson

"It's My Brain"

I'm pretty sure you've gotten where I'm going by now – forced schooling (private or public schooling) is a violation of kids' rights. In this case, it is their pirate right to sail the seas of information-discovery on their own time and at their own pleasure.

Kids understand by the age of about six that people grow up to have jobs one day. By the age of 8, many or most free kids are already thinking about what they might like to do "when they grow up". One of my daughter's free friends realized at age 7 that her absolute love of animals and taking care of them meant that she would probably be a veterinarian. She has now picked out the college she'll be going to for her veterinary degree.

My own free daughter was pretty sure by the age of 10 that she wanted to be an architect, and by the age of 12 was "pretty darn sure". Both girls immersed themselves in those two fields of information without a single word of motivation or suggestion by me or others.

Not all free kids figure out their chosen professions so quickly. One free boy chose not to learn to read until he was 11 years old – he ended up being a computer programmer with a business of his own by the age of 17. With free kids, you just never know – and it's none of our business, outside of being excited for them and lovingly helping them whenever they may ask. It's THEIR exciting life.

Another thing I've seen in free kids is that they are mad about governments telling them when they can get a job. My own daughter complained that she couldn't get a job until she was 15. She was also upset that she couldn't drive until she was 16. Free kids feel in control of their lives and don't like being told what they CAN'T do. They want to jump into the world and DO things on their own time schedules. They aren't obnoxious about it. They just want to get on with their lives as they see fit – not as OTHERS see fit.

And they certainly don't want to sit in a classroom, not of their choosing, and be told to sit in one place and be quiet and learn what they're told to learn and go to the bathroom when they are told it's OK to go to the bathroom and take tests on the information inside THEIR heads, which is THEIR information. "Why do they get to know what's inside my head? It's MY brain!"

And what a brain it is!

The One-Size-Fits-All Bootcamp

And that brain isn't just acquiring knowledge at a break-neck speed. It's also trying to figure out what profession or career to get into – which is much more difficult to do if the child is being forced into a school setting during the week instead of exploring with their own free will.

Some websites count how many careers there are in the world. Those I visited agreed that there are over 12,000 "popular" careers to be had in our world – and probably more than 100,000 total, if you include such things as Pet Groomer and Philatelist and Butterfly Collector and Storm Chaser and Rocketship Builder and Doll Collector and Professional Gamer and Dog Food Tester and Skyscraper Window Washer and Zoo Artificial Inseminator and Quantum Physicist and Professional Reader and Business Comedian and Non-Destructive Tester and Vegetation Tattoo Artist and Sword-Cutting Hair Stylist and Consultant for Marketing Consultants and Jane Austen Reader and Cockpit Voiceover Expert.

This list goes on endlessly. Capitalism is the ultimate baby-maker of careers. There's something for seemingly everyone. And since our careers are so important and give us pride and self-esteem and happiness, kids need to be free during their formative years to explore the world of 100,000+ potentially exciting careers. They shouldn't be stuck in a stodgy classroom when the pirate urge for greatness is strongest.

And to the point, no public or private education during the formative years could ever hope to train kids for any of the above. Instead, coercive education has the jaw-dropping-boring-endgame of providing a "well-rounded education" – whatever that's supposed to mean. (Personally, I like people who specialize in things and have a little edge.) Even if schools could provide a "well-rounded education", who's to say that that would be a good thing? And who's to say that any kid would WANT such a yawner? Einstein and the eminent physicist Marie Curie were not "well-rounded".

"Nothing in life is to be feared; it is only to be understood." Marie Curie.

Potential rocketship builders may not give a hoot about history or literature or chemistry or "social studies" (perhaps the most boring title for a class in the history of classes) or "physical education" (never quite understood how that is an "education") or arts studies. They might want algebra and other higher math, but 99% of kids don't NEED algebra and other higher math to do their eventual jobs that they choose. Algebra, then, would be a waste of TIME.

And do the rocketship builders REALLY need to read Alexandre Dumas' "The Three Musketeers" or Caesar's history of his campaigns in Gaul or a book on the social plight of loom workers in England in the 18th century or remember the 47th element on the Periodic Table or learn art-brushing skills or play a sport with others they don't know in a sport they didn't choose?

The same thing goes for all the other 100,000+ careers in life. There simply is no such thing as a one-size-fits-all, 12-year bootcamp for those careers. And there is no good reason for a so-called "well-rounded education" when people need SPECIFIC information only about what they are interested in. A "well-rounded" education is simply a cut-and-paste hodge-podge of subjects that some busybodies contrived, frankly, to keep children under the thumb of elitists, who allegedly know better than the children what to do with the children's lives.

Personally, in high school I was forced to read Jane Austen, Shakespeare and Dickens, among others. All three bored me to tears. Now I love Austen and Shakespeare tremendously (after doing enough actual living to understand them). But reading Dickens is still the worst of times! My point is that nobody can know when I or anybody else is ready for something or will ever be interested in something. Only the individual knows that, including children. There can be no artificial time and place and subject-set for life-learning.

Life isn't supposed to be a bootcamp. It's supposed to be a thrilling adventure.

Don't Know Much About Hiiiistory

And let's not be fooled by schooling elitists who toss cute clich s and canards at us to justify mandatory formal schooling. To be successful and happy in life, kids don't have to take formal classes in anything, especially such standards as history or literature or chemistry or algebra or "social studies" – or even basic math or reading or writing. Here's a list of some clich s and canards by the elitists:

1) "Those who don't know history are doomed to repeat it." No. What these unfortunate souls mean is that if our kids don't study the mistakes in history, they'll grow up and make the same mistakes. But that isn't true. All we need to know is what is right and wrong. The examples of right and wrong are a daily occurrence for kids. They don't need to study Caesar to figure out that bullies and dictators are on a very bad Path. And, frankly, they don't need to even study our Founding Fathers to determine that they have rights to their lives – and that government needs to stay out of our business.

2) "Only the very weak-minded refuse to be influenced by literature and poetry." This quote by Cassandra Clare epitomizes the elitist mindset of the schoolers, who believe that a formal education in literature is necessary to give depth, meaning and understanding to our lives. I happen to love literature, and I know a lot of people who do, but a person could go their entire lives never doing serious reading and live well and fully.

3) "Don't trust atoms. They make up everything." OK, that's a joke. Couldn't help myself. But it's also a joke that anyone could possibly believe that kids need chemistry or physics to get by in life or to help them "learn how to think", which is the canard used for almost all formal schooling classes. No, kids already have a 3-pound brain that knows exactly how to think – and frankly, finds its own formula for happiness and information-gathering.

4) "It's the integrated study of the social sciences and humanities to promote civic competence." Confused? Me, too. That is the definition of "social studies" by the ominous-sounding National Council for Social Studies. Bet that's a fun place to work! What that quote really means is that our kids need to "learn" how to be good little boys and girls in society, instead of free, independent people who demand their own rights and honor others' rights to their lives. Michelle Herczog, the president of the ominous NCSS actually had the lunacy to state in April 2015 that is was necessary "to have the glue of social studies to make responsible citizens". What she really means is government-stamped obedient citizens. No, it is not necessary to take a class to be responsible. It is only necessary to grow up in a home with at least one Happy Oak Tree. And it is certainly not the government schools' jobs to be churning out "citizens"

of any sort – though they are indeed churning out obedient and rebellious kids by the millions.

5) "What do you call the little rivers that flow into the Nile? … Juveniles." Couldn't resist another joke. Geography is another joke class. It isn't needed in life. It's simply another class that allows someone to get paid for imparting information that kids will or will not learn by themselves, according to their goals. Few jobs require us to know the capital of Burkina Faso. My daughter decided one day at age 11, for whatever reason, to learn all the states of the United States. She Googled for "quiz games" on U.S. States. Found one that looked fun. In less than two days of playing, she knew the location and shape of all the states and half their capitals. Kids do that. They don't need outside brain-probers (teachers) telling them to learn the location of Basque highlanders or whatever else. Geography is NOT necessary for life. And, BTW, free kids start Googling for information around the age of 4 or 5. They are pirate rocketships from that day forward.

6) "Rah Rah Rah". That was the head cheerleader's answer to the question "Do you know your Three Rs"? As a young kid, I was just as confused when I heard the phrase "Three Rs" and then saw the words. The phrase was first used in a speech about 200 years ago in England, so the phonetic sounds made sense, of course, but the joke, unfortunately is on kids again. Children don't need any Rs rammed down their throats. They learn reading, 'riting and 'rithmatic as easy as one, two, three. Free kids learn these simple subjects quickly from the age of 4 to the age of 12, depending on their interest in them. These subjects of formal schooling are simply in place to provide sinecure positions for people wishing to keep children obediently in their seats, bored out of their minds – and "well-rounded". Kids do, however, require Three Rs from others: Respect, Rights, Recognition.

"Well-Rounded"

Since I've been mentioning "well-rounded", let's run with that for a moment.

As a kid, I learned more interesting things about the world by watching the news or listening to my parents or talking with other kids. I learned what was going on with the government, with other nations, with some of the history of all that, with what books I wanted to read, with insects, with animals, with sports, with other activities, with diplomacy, with judgment, with fairness, with games, with math, with grammar. In modern times, kids learn even more via the Internet – potentially 10 times more quickly.

My "unschooled" daughter knows virtually every pertinent fact about the Twin Towers' tragically falling, and yet she could not possibly remember it. She knows about the latest private ventures into space simply by paying attention to things and being interested. She loves anything related to Sherlock Holmes stories simply by first being fascinated with a TV series and then following up herself. Same with Anne of Green Gables and many other books and shows.

She learned how to read and write by herself by asking me questions and by playing online gaming between the ages of 6 and 9 and by watching me read to her – and just paying attention to things that she was interested in at the grocery store and on the highway and in the livingroom and on her phone or iPad.

Kids learn to read and write as easily as they learn to speak a language. They don't need "school" for any of those things. In fact, school gets in the way of their natural inclination to learn excitedly at their own pace.

Kathryn and her other "unschooled" friends have always been stunningly savvy about the world – so much so that I often caught myself asking them, "How in the world did you KNOW that?" At the age of six, one of her young friends used the word "levitate". I asked her, "How did you know that, girl?" She nonchalantly said she was watching a magic trick on YouTube. Amazing. THAT is how they learn!

Nowadays, free kids are remarkably "well-rounded" (in their interests) simply by living life in an Internet age, though I think a better word might be "eclectic". They have a vast and eclectic understanding of a wide array of fields of knowledge – without a speck of schooling.

Frankly, modern schools are jokes (that's the kids' word for them) for this age and time. Schools always have been a joke, but it's especially so with the advent of Wikipedia, Google, YouTube, BuzzFeed, online gaming, online courses, free online foreign language learning (which I personally did), Facebook, Pinterest (my daughter has several Pin folders with her favorite clothing styles and people and architecture), and much more.

My daughter and her friends have chosen to take a-la-carte classes on Greek gods, literature, chess, art, dancing, martial arts, Lyra, gymnastics, dramatic plays, silks, pottery, cursive writing, algebra (my daughter was curious and learned its basics on "unknowns" in two hours, like most kids can if it's made clear), the stock market (their team won a regional contest on stock market predictions at the age of 11), fashion, and much much more.

I'm not bragging on my daughter and her friends. That's just what free kids DO. They are highly motivated and self-directed and don't have time for "schooling" designed and run by strangers or even family members. They have no patience for a cookie-cutter approach to learning in a 12-year bootcamp desk. Life is too exciting and wonderful to be confined to a desk for one-hour snooze-fests – and then have one's free nighttime pirate ship assaulted by someone else's demand for "homework".

An artificial line-up of subjects contrived by outside "experts" with virtually no thought given to future career interests does not make a child well-rounded. It brow-beats children into obedience to others. It makes a child lose interest in what THEY want to do in life, to lose some of their free will, to lose that glorious joy for living that young children have before they step inside the bootcamps.

And worst of all, it's a direct and obvious violation of their right to their lives.

Homeschool Bootcamps

It's terrific that millions of U.S. parents have gotten fed up with the robo-droid, test-taking mental nightmare that is "public school" and withdrawn their kids from those bootcamps and brought them home. About a quarter-million of those parents have even taken the courageous step of letting their kids learn completely freely about the world on their own. No curriculum. That movement is called "unschooling".

Unschooling parents don't usually understand that their kids have a "right" to be unschooled, as this book discusses, but they still sense that their children need to be set free. Good on those parents! Hopefully those parents will now be full Oak Trees honoring their kids' rights to full self-governance of their lives.

Unfortunately, the rest of the millions of parents who brought their children home from bootcamp are now committing the same violation of rights against their kids as was previously happening in the bootcamps. The parents are "homeschooling" – meaning the parents are forcing education artificially on their children at home, whether the kids agree to it or not. This is, of course, most likely a "fuzzier" bootcamp than the brick-and-mortar one down the road, but it is still a bootcamp, designed, unfortunately, to "impart" on the children's minds what the parents (instead of administrators) wish the kids to learn and do.

The curriculum these parents impose is often based on oppressive government regulations, but those regulations can easily be handled without forcing curriculums upon the children. I recommend joining one of the hundreds of unschooling lists around the United States to find out how you can stay away from imposing curriculums on your children and still abide by intrusive government regulations. These lists also help you "let go" of your habit of dictating your kids' education.

If you need help learning how to work the laws in your state as an unschooler, you can contact the Home School Legal Defense Foundation (http://www.hslda.org). They are magnificent at helping you not only understand your rights but also to help out legally with any issues that may arise. Though they began as an aide and advocate of homeschoolers, they now help unschoolers, too. Good on them!

Bootcamps Are NOT Child Daycare

It's a busy world. We have busy lives. Both parents are often working. The tendency of such households (or single-parent households) is to find a daycare facility to "put" the kids in while the parents are working. And that place is usually public or private schooling bootcamps for kids over 4. (BTW, I think actual daycare facilities for very young children are a nightmare of intrusion into kids' rights, not to mention germ factories. Daycares have dozens of outrageous rules, such as marching in lines to go outdoors and forced sharing and not swinging to high, etc.)

Daycare-schooling parents don't mean harm to their children. In fact, many think they are doing the best for their children. But such schools, as I've said already, are probably the WORST place your children can go during the day.

So-called public schools are obedience and mind-warping machines that have gotten even worse with so-called "Common Core". They violate the rights of kids to run their own lives. Not to mention that they are simply no longer safe – and no parent, frankly, can feel in good conscience about sending their beloved child to such dangerous quarters.

It isn't our children's fault if both parents are working, so why should we force them into public-school daycare because we didn't plan well for their future?

Private schools are a lot more safe, but they also are not daycare facilities, and they violate the children's rights to self-determination.

Unschooling

Virtually all parents reading this book and agreeing with me on the rights of children may now find yourselves in a pickle – where does your child go during the day while you're at work?

Here are my three recommendations (with your child's approval, of course):

1) Find an unschooling family nearby who takes in other unschool kids and charges you very little for taking in your kids during the day. You can find these families on the unschooling lists I mentioned earlier. I've found the unschooling parents to be largely wonderful people who care about kids' freedoms.
2) Find a family member or friend who is home during the day and completely agrees with you about your children's right to be free and will honor that when you are at work. Work out something with them that is beneficial to you both.
3) Find an unschooling "school" nearby. There are usually two kinds of these "schools". One is simply buildings where unschooling parents get together and offer classes on subjects, and unschooling kids take the classes voluntarily at a modest charge. The other has been around for more than 40 years. It is called Sudbury Schools. These are essentially unschooling centers with computers and big yards and a bunch of books and objects for kids to play with and learn from. The kids are completely free to explore things themselves and join other free kids on projects or whatever they desire. There is usually a modest annual tuition. You can look up "Sudbury school" on Wikipedia to learn more about these wonderful centers for free kids.

If you Google "unschooling", you'll find all sorts of information, including the wonderful website www.lifelearningmagazine.com. It's not a perfect site because it doesn't directly promote the "rights" of children, but it does focus well on unschooling, life learning, free-range learning and natural learning – all of which are based on kids learning for themselves via their pirate lives and loving parents.

Raising and Teaching Kids is Not a Career

The title of this section may get a few hackles up. But if kids can teach themselves and learn by themselves and be autonomous by around the age of 8 (as free kids are), then the "raising" of kids just got a whole lot simpler. And it IS simpler with free, responsible kids. Us parents are Oak Tree Care-Friends who set bad Paths to good Paths, but we are largely hands-off on their little pirate lives – outside of doing things with them and taking care of obvious occasional needs.

The first two years of a child's life is the only truly intense and seriously hands-on (breasts-on) period for a parent – often the mother at this stage. But even then, most of the parenting is downtime while the baby sleeps up to 18 hours a day and the toddler sleeps up to 12 hours a day.

And we've already established that there's no teaching or "guiding" children – only loving interactions. So, what is a mother or father to do if there is not a whole lot TO do? The answer is to at least have an avocation, a part-time career or serious interest that requires the use of one's mind and actions to get self-fulfillment out of one's life. I've seen too many parents, especially moms, wither on the vine of "child-raising". Those days should be over – for good.

With the dawn of the mechanical age in the home in the 20th century, household chores are no longer achingly time-consuming, and all kids over the age of five can do their share of the chores and SHOULD be doing their share of the chores. So parents really don't have a lot to do in a free home environment. Raising free kids is a TIMESAVER!

So with all that extra free time, we can either be couch potatoes or we can find meaningful work. I vote for the latter and for a productive, vibrant lifestyle – which gives us full self-esteem and the confidence to be the Happy Oak Tree. We can't be happy or Oak Trees if we are idle. Life should be pleasantly busy and we should be in the pirate mix of it all.

I don't know who came up with the term "homemaker", but outside of big estates ("Gone With the Wind"?) that require an actual overseer of accounts and constant upkeep, there's simply not enough to do to "stay busy".

The only exception to this, I think, would be parents who have a lot of kids in succession. But even then, the older kids can take care of themselves in a free environment, and the "succession" only lasts so long. It is true that we are constantly taking the older kids to events and practices (I think I logged at least 30,000 miles!), but that can be incorporated into an active lifestyle with a part-time or full-time career – and you can join with other good families for "relays" on the transport.

"But What If They Turn Out Bad?"

I've talked with dozens of people (maybe hundreds) about raising my "wild child" daughter in honor of her rights. The two questions I've gotten almost every time are: 1) "So you LET her do anything?" and 2) "But What If She Turns Out Bad?"

I can't help but smile when I get these queries, and my daughter smiled as she got older when I told her about these queries.

The reason Kathryn and I smiled is that I wasn't "LETTING" her do anything, and it didn't occur to her to be "bad". At first, she was confused that adults could be so "clueless" about her and her life. I had to explain to her many times that other kids just weren't raised the way she was. She knew it was and is her right to do with her life as she pleases, including not going to school, and that nobody LETS other people have rights, because they get them at birth.

It would be like someone walking up to an adult and saying, "Do you LET your friends do anything with their lives?" It sounds crazy when you say it that way – because it is crazy. Us parents don't let our kids be free. They have a RIGHT to be free, and all we can do is either HONOR that right or not honor that right.

The other question about "turning out bad" has more depth and more psychological implications. The implicit comment in the question is: "A child can't turn out good without guidance and outside direction and commands. They have to be controlled and to abide by a list of rules to be good and not turn out bad." This isn't true for kids, any more than it is true of us adults. We don't need a master.

A deeper issue with these questions is the feeling of responsibility that these parents feel they have for how their children turn out. One of the purposes of this book is to show how we completely let go of that feeling, to honor our kids' rights to determine their own paths – and eventually be good or bad on their own merit.

I admit to having the same worry when I decided before Kathryn's birth to completely honor her right to freedom for her whole life. I finally had to have a serious talk with myself, basically saying, "Look, she's got a right to be whatever she wants. You're doing the right thing, and that is truly what matters. You'll always be there for her and you'll love her with all your heart, and you'll talk to her all the time when she feels like it. But in the end, it's not YOUR responsibility for how she turns out. It's hers. That's what freedom means. It means the freedom to turn out awesome or the freedom to not be awesome. Let it go!"

When I was in my 20s and early 30s, I was very much into literature, history, drama and art, so I also had to have a talk with myself about letting go on trying to teach her stuff that I knew and that I thought might be good for her. I'm glad she ended up liking some of those things, but it would've been fine if she didn't. The great thing is that since I didn't try to coax her or hint to her about what she "ought" to do, I knew that whatever she WAS doing, she truly loved doing it – and she DID.

I cannot take credit for how awesome she's become, and no parent can truly take credit for their kids' awesomeness – except in one regard. You can take full credit for honoring their right to be free to be awesome – and you can know that it was YOU who honored that right. Then simply bask in your awesome child – and enjoy the deep friendship and trust that is the result.

One final point on "turning out bad". I've not seen even ONE unmotivated free child yet. They are all extremely motivated and interesting, and they honor other people's rights to be free and quirky (which we all are). When a child is free to explore their pirate life, it simply doesn't get boring for them. They've always got something they want to do – unlike many "schooled" kids and helicoptered kids, who are, unfortunately, often apathetic and a little lazy.

It doesn't even seem to occur to free kids to be "bad" or "turn out bad". They've got so much they want to do with their lives – and that is a good thing.

College – The Pit of Despair and Debt

Another tagline that may get some hackles up. Colleges have turned to junk, and the "college track" isn't necessary for 90% of kids, who will be getting technical jobs or other jobs that require only on-the-job training or an apprenticeship or short technical classes, but not multi-year degrees. More than half of 20-somethings coming out of college now aren't even getting jobs in their chosen careers.

And the colleges themselves have become abysmal, including the "Ivy League" big boys. The curriculums are divided into thirds: 1) actual courses that are pertinent to your degree plan and that you need to learn; 2) mandatory classes to give you an alleged "social responsibility" and make you "well-rounded" (there's that phrase again!); 3) and "elective" classes that have absolutely nothing to do with your career plan and could be learned quickly on Wikipedia.

Junk! Two-thirds of the classes have nothing to do with what you want to do with your life – but you still pay for them.

Expensive junk!

College has become, frankly, a costly means for colleges to get rich and employ professors who largely just hand out textbooks for students to get their information from. Students walk away with a big debt and only a rudimentary understanding of their career field that they probably could've learned by themselves.

But.

But "public schools" have gotten so bad and are churning out such large quantities of kids "who memorize well for tests" and who lack the ability to think on their feet and think well (a problem that free kids don't have) that many employers are afraid to hire high-school grads even for executive secretary positions. In fact, colleges and employers are now practically begging for teens who haven't had any formal education (unschoolers) because they CAN think on their feet and are highly motivated.

The colleges know the problem with high school grads. They know that employers are often frightened of them. So many colleges are raising their costs and offering essentially "paper degrees". Employers may still not like the college student's lack of ability to think well and be independent, but the college grads at least showed a dedication to put more information in their heads, and employers like that.

That said, we still come back to 90% of jobs not needing degrees. So why are so many teens going to college? Because parents are pushing them to go, and because some teens simply don't want to go to work yet (party time!) after 12 dreadful years of "schooling", and because having a degree is considered prestigious by many parents and kids.

Maybe it's time to rethink the "college track" – or at least be realistic about what it entails. It is not "prestigious" to waste one's time, and there are many institutions now offering good information online at very low prices.

A college degree? … "I do not think it means what you think it means".

Schooling Schmooling

I thought I'd throw in the list below, so we can all see what great people did with little or no formal education. Life isn't about "schooling". It's about drive, ambition, learning as you go, creativity, freedom. Here's a list of 20 truly great people who never went to school or who dropped out of school.

1) **Albert Einstein** – high school dropout
2) **Mark Twain** – dropped out after fifth grade
3) **Steve Jobs** – dropped out of college after six months
4) **Henry Ford** – no schooling
5) **William Shakespeare** – no school past age 13
6) **Abraham Lincoln** – no formal education at all
7) **Abigail Adams** – no formal education at all
8) **Andre Agassi** – 9th grade dropout
9) **Dean Martin** – high school dropout
10) **John D. Rockefeller** – world's 1st billionaire was high school dropout
11) **Ellen DeGeneres** – "I didn't go to no college"
12) **Andrew Carnegie** – elementary school dropout
13) **Winston Churchill** – flunked sixth grade
14) **Leonardo da Vinci** – no formal education; apprenticed as youth
15) **George Washington** – elementary school dropout
16) **Frank Lloyd Wright** – high school dropout
17) **Annie Leibovitz** – no formal education; "I had to teach myself"
18) **Bill Gates** – college dropout

19) **Thomas Edison** – elementary school dropout; teacher called him "addled"
20) **Lucille Ball** – high school dropout

I Think, Therefore I know

You've heard me talk a lot about how amazing the minds of children are, so I thought I'd put together a brief list of some of the most difficult things they learn all by themselves (from their surroundings) by about the age of 8, just as an example of their greatness – and their ability to handle life themselves. Here it is:

1) **Morality** – the difference between good and bad
2) **Gravity** – and that things fall "harder" from higher places
3) **Water** has three states – liquid, gas, solid
4) **Ownership** – humans have their OWN property
5) **Intelligence** – humans are much smarter than other animals
6) **Fairness** – people DESERVE to be treated according to their actions
7) **Honesty** – being true to oneself and to the world feels good
8) **Work** – doing constructive things is satisfying
9) **Words** – they represent things in the universe
10) **Boundaries** – there's a limit to everything
11) **Reciprocity** – you need good friends and good friends need you
12) **Consequences** – all actions and thoughts have implications
13) **Money** – it represents work and is used to pay for others' work
14) **Art** – it is a unique expression of one's self
15) **Quid pro quo** – I scratch your back and you scratch my back
16) **Time** – a human invention for planning (and birthdays!)
17) **Integrity** – we can be proud when we figure things out and act on it
18) **Independence** – it's satisfying to figure things out all by yourself
19) **Confidence** – I can do things all by myself
20) **Freedom** – I love it when nobody is telling my what to do

Eight-year-old children may not know all of the words above, but if they could put into words how they are feeling and what they've learned, those would be some of the big words. And, of course, by the age of 8, they've learned hundreds of principles (fairness is good, etc.) and more than 10,000 concepts (words). Such as:

Sharp, dull, hot, cold, long, short, fat, skinny, soft, hard, rough, smooth, smart, dumb, mean, nice, quiet, loud, fast, slow, thick, thin, breakable, bendable, high, low, safe, dangerous, winning, losing, light, dark, rising, falling, shy, talkative, fair, unfair, self, others, gas, liquid, numbers, letters, strong, weak, good, bad, life, death, movement, stillness, plants, animals, air, space, sticky, clean, health, disease, music, dance, angry, happy, friends, enemies, peace, war, love, hate, constructing, destroying, tasting, hearing, seeing, feeling, smelling.

I've barely scratched the surface of children's remarkable minds. By the age of 8, free kids learn all of the above and a thousands times more by themselves – with their five senses, their minds, and simple conversations with us loved ones.

Even if we had a right to force them into school, it wouldn't be just fruitless – it would also be condescending and harmful. It would be like saying, "OK, yeah, I see that you've learned a TON of things by yourself, but, um, you really do need somebody else telling you what to learn and when to learn and how to learn."

No. Life is the ultimate teacher.

School's out forever!

Chapter Seventeen

Me, Myself and I
It's All About You You You

"Love yourself first, and everything else falls into line. You really have to love yourself to get anything done in this world." – Lucille Ball (Lucy)

As much as we dearly love our children, we have to love ourselves even more. I've unfortunately heard many women (especially) say, "I put the needs of my children before my needs." Goodness! That is a recipe for disaster in any relationship, whether it's with our kids, our spouses, our friends, or our families. It isn't heroic or brave or noble to put others' needs over ours – despite what the pastor or the neighbor or the doctor or an aunt or the president or anyone else says.

We shouldn't be expecting pats on the back for having or raising our kids – nor should we want the pats. We WANTED to have them, to enrich our lives, so doing things for them isn't a sacrifice or "putting us out" or a chore. If doing things for our kids were a chore, we could say the same thing about our adult relationships and the work that they take to stay real and meaningful.

We should be having and raising kids because we want to satisfy US – because it is something that makes US happy. Sure, we want to help our kids out when they need it, so they can make themselves happy – and therefore make US happy to be around them and love them. In the end, it's really about US … US … US. Some people may think that sounds selfish, but it's true – it's self-full. We can't make others happy unless we are happy first.

Before we can take care of others' needs and say "I love you" with full meaning to them, we have to first take care of our self-full lives – we have to take care of "I". We have to sail down our own adult pirate paths before we can truly enjoy and nurture our kids' pirate paths. "Sacrificing" for others turns us into sacrificial animals, whom others can take advantage of – because they know we're putting THEM first.

What I mean by putting them first is, for example:

1) You do what they want to do even when you don't want to do it. (This is OK if being with them is more important than what you wanted to do.)

2) You let them run over you sometimes because you don't want to "cause trouble" with the relationship or "put them out".
3) You regularly get them something that they could (should) get themselves.
4) You don't mention things you're concerned about because you don't want to put them in a bad mood or you are afraid of a confrontation.
5) You don't show your own anger or sorrow because you don't want to "bring them down". But kids trust us more if we trust them with our grief.
6) You let them make a lot noise because stopping them will upset them.
7) You don't say "what's on your chest" when they're in a pitiful mood – because you're afraid it will make them more pitiful.
8) You don't disagree with them out loud, keeping your thoughts to yourself – because you think they can't take it or it will make them mad.
9) You don't go out on a date because your child doesn't like the person.
10) You don't buy something for yourself because your child doesn't like it.

Doing any of the above or other self-denial things leads to resentment, frustration, anger and moodiness in you – because you're denying your self-fullness. You aren't seeking your own joy ALL THE TIME out of life, so you're sacrificing instead of being the self-full Happy Oak Tree – instead of doing what you want to do and dealing with the situation.

It's No Sacrifice

The great American author Ayn Rand called sacrifice "giving up a greater value for a lesser value". I like that definition a lot. It gets to the point. In the above list of 10 sacrifices, you gave up your own self-full happiness and goals for somebody else's goals or alleged well-being. Women have been told for centuries that they must do this – commit this sort of hara-kiri sacrifice, and now men who stay at home to raise kids are being told the same thing.

But, ironically, people are happier when they are NOT sacrificing. When we are doing what we want to do all the time, we are happy. It makes other happy people glad to be around us, too, and it makes angry people or manipulative people miserable to be around us because they can't make us sacrifice our own happiness and desires. And that's a good thing!

If we are Happy Oak Trees running down our pirate paths alongside our children, then if someone wishes us to change who we are or pretend that we like something we don't or walk on eggshells around them or do their bidding, then we HAPPILY decline – and thoughtfully explain ourselves, if necessary.

But I need to clarify "sacrifice" a little more.

We are never sacrificing if we TRULY want to do something – no matter if it changes our previous plans or is a messy thing or a long-term thing or a difficult thing. As long as it is a "greater" value in the moment than what we had previously planned, then it is a good thing, and not a sacrificial thing.

For example, if we truly and deeply love our children, it's no sacrifice to stay home with a sick child instead of going to that big costume party we've been anticipating for a month. Yeah, the costume party would've been a ball, but soothing your adorable child through a hard time is MORE important in the moment. You couldn't be happy at the party, knowing that your sickly child was at home with somebody else, no matter how caring that other person is. Your greater value is to be with your lovely child. There will be other costume parties. It's no sacrifice – even if your friends and family praise you for your "sacrifice".

So, how do we know we are not sacrificing – that we're not giving up a greater value for a lesser value? We have to KNOW ourselves and KNOW what we want and be self-full all the time and be honest with ourselves and stand by our integrity. We have to want to be happy! I think it's even a good thing to say to ourselves, "I love my dear children, and I will do almost anything for them, but I love myself even more, and I must be happy. I won't sacrifice myself for them – or for anybody. I will remain true to myself always."

It is impossible to please anyone else and hold their feet to the fire, when necessary, if we don't love ourselves first and hold our feet to the fire on our own behavior. And we cannot be Oak Trees in our lives if we put ANYBODY before ourselves – our love of ourselves. Our love of our LIVES. I'm not talking about "self-absorption" here. I'm just talking about taking care of yourself and focusing on what you need from life.

Some people call this "selfish". But it's not selfish to want to LIVE – to live a life full of meaning to us, of goals that are accomplished, of work we are proud of, of friends we earned and trust, of daily joys and activities, of independence, of freedom, of courage, of steadfast action.

Our kids are obviously majorly important to us and we spend a heck of a lot of time with them and work on them, but that is VERY different from putting them ABOVE our own happiness. They are not frail little things that require our sacrifice. They are budding pirates on a course to somewhere only they can know. The people and things in our lives that are very important to us cannot become BIGGER than us. That's putting it all backwards. They are an important PART of us – not larger than us. And the parts simply make up the whole that is "I".

In every single situation in our lives with others, we should ask ourselves, "Is this what I want, and is this good for me and/or will it benefit my longterm happiness?" In other words, being self-full is NOT hedonism. It is thoughtful reflection on what is good for YOU to prosper. If it is good for you, no matter what it is, then you should do it. If it isn't, then you should not – no matter what 20 million other people might say to you.

Life is not about what others think of us. It is only about what we want – what we must have to be happy, and not be a sacrificial animal.

"I" ... Am the Oak Tree

People who sacrifice themselves for others can't be happy or be a Happy Oak Tree. They've already made it clear that what others want is more important than what they want, so their fallback position is to cater to the whims and desires of others. So when those "others" go on bad Paths, well, "Who am I to judge?"

I'm going to be a little bit harsh here, but what those sacrificial people are really saying is, "I'm too much of a coward to live my own life and be strong and stand up for myself and be happy and firm." It is a lot easier to cop out of judgment and firmness than to be an Oak Tree, but the repercussions for copping out actually make life a LOT harder, with people regularly taking advantage of us.

When this happens, a lot of people (mainly women) become "victims" of others' remarks and demands, and then they play victimhood like a Stradivarius. Being a victim then becomes their raison d' tre for life – their reason for living.

"I don't do damsel in distress very well. It's hard for me to play a victim." – Scarlett Johansson.

"Damsels in distress" cannot be Oak Trees for their children. Victims are not good role models, any more than authoritarian parents are good role models. Victims and authoritarians cannot be Oak Trees because they are already on bad Paths themselves, and the children see this – they see everything!

But if children see that your "I" is the most important thing to you, then their "I" will be the most important thing to them. They won't be victims either. They will be Oak Trees. You will joyfully thrive together along separate pirate Paths holding hands and respecting each other's self-full discovery.

Kids may be the world's harshest critics. This is probably why so many parents try to control kids. They see the kids judging the parents' bad Paths, and that reproach is not pleasant. But we should welcome and enjoy the judgment of our kids and others, because we've got our s**t together. We should be judging ourselves resolutely and ensuring that we're staying self-full and focused on "I".

So, how do we get to the self-full "I" and Happy Oak Tree if we aren't there already – if we've got some anxiety in us all the time or we feel a little bit off-balance about handling our kids and life?

Here's what we have to do:

1) Recognize that our **happiness** is the goal of life
2) Recognize that **the universe** is understandable ("it is what it is")
3) Recognize and respect our 3-pound brain – and know that its **rationality** can handle anything in life, even our emotions
4) Be **productive** (have a good career, good health and good friends)
5) Be **independent** (think for ourselves)
6) Be **honest** (never turn our heads from the truth – and speak the truth)
7) Good **judgment** (judging ourselves and others fairly always)
8) Have **integrity** (organize our thoughts and act on them)
9) Have and enjoy our rightful **pride** in ourselves
10) Enjoy our **emotions** and feelings that we get by doing all the above

The Pursuit of Happiness

I've always thought it interesting and ingenious that Thomas Jefferson didn't say that people have a right to "happiness". He said we have a right to the PURSUIT of happiness, with the understanding, of course, that happiness is the goal of life. The pursuit is a given, right? After all, the opposite would be that we have a right to the pursuit of misery. Ha! I suppose we do, but that isn't what we OUGHT to do.

TJ was talking about self-full happiness. What the American revolutionaries did against Britain was not an exercise in sacrifice. They had a higher value than obedience to "the usurpations" of the Brits. Their value was freedom, and they were willing to die for it, rather than be the subjects of "despotism".

The same goes for our singular lives every day. Will we pursue our own happiness, with our children as very high values, but not higher than our own value? Will we live freely as our own pirates, taking care of others we care about, but not doing it to the point that it stops us from caring for ourselves?

Will we proclaim happiness, and its pursuit, to be the highest value of our lives all the time – in the home, in the car, in the workplace, at family gatherings, everywhere?! If we care about ourselves and our children, we must proclaim this – to be the Happy Oak Tree in all aspects of our life. The alternative is anxiety, anger, dread, tentativeness and victimhood – and that's no way to live!

"We are taught you must blame your father, your sisters, your brothers, the school, the teachers – but never blame yourself. It's never your fault. But it's always your fault, because if you wanted to change, you're the one who has got to change."
– Katharine Hepburn

It Is What It Is

Everybody who has had kids older than 5 knows that kids are some of our biggest watchers, biggest admirers and biggest critics. They see EVERYTHING – every contradiction, every loving moment, every fairness or unfairness, every weakness, every strength, every lie, every truth.

Our status as the Happy Oak Tree depends on truth and strength of character. Obviously and primarily, our happiness itself depends on these characteristics, but we're talking about kids here, and they judge all the time, even when they are unfortunately told that they should not.

This makes the "just the facts, ma'am" approach to life all the more important. The facts of life are simply "it is what it is". Facts are good. Facts are real. They are life itself. If we veer from facts, we pay the price – such as getting burned by a friend who has shown themselves to be a liar, but we stayed friends anyway. Frankly, we deserved to get burned for not sticking to the facts and being self-full enough to get the heck out of the relationship. That's the cost of avoiding facts, being irrational.

The vital fact-based approach to life extends to EVERYTHING – even religion. If we are to maintain our mental credibility with ourselves and our kids, we must question everything we've been told and see if "it is what it is".

Religion is based on "faith", not facts. ("Ours is not to reason why".) This confuses children and, frankly, every person I've ever met, even priests, who have their "moments of doubt". I would imagine they do, since "faith" means "believe it because somebody said so or it is written, even if it doesn't make any sense". This is, frankly, a slap in the face to any pirate mind in search of the facts of life and the reasons for things happening – and it undermines the Oak Tree, who is supposed to make sense.

I'm no longer religious, but growing up a Christian with my Christian friends, we would sometimes get together after church and scratch our heads, basically, at what the preacher said or what our parents said. For example, we never could figure out how a "god" would send its immortal son (who may also be the god AND "father" AND a "ghost") to Earth to be murdered by the very people the god was supposed to be trying to get closer to – but then the murdered son would rise and head back to heaven, as if not dead at all and getting the heck out of Dodge. Huh?

It used to scare my friends and I a good bit that our parents would sit obediently and quietly in church while the preacher was saying these things "with authority" – and other things, like people are "fallen" and "bad" and "selfish" and "have the devil in them" and needed Jesus to fix all that. We didn't like the fact that our "fix" was supposed to come from outside us and that we only had to "believe" in order to get "fixed". Seemed weird, and it seemed like our lives weren't our own and we were so "bad" that we couldn't fix our lives ourselves.

Us kids were always watching and analyzing. That's what kids do until their parents and others insist that they believe in something without facts. At this point the kids will probably be obedient or rebel silently or be a little bit of both. But the one primary thing they will all do, consciously or unconsciously, is lower their respect for those who INSIST on believing and surrendering their mental faculties to anything – including religion.

At this point, the parental Oak Tree begins withering, losing its credibility. Happy Oak Trees cannot insist that kids see that any of their bad Paths "are what they are" if the Oak Tree will not see what "is what it is".

My point in the above is not to make people stop being religious, though that would be good for them and their kids. It is to show that being religious undermines your own confidence in the realness of the universe and life, and undermines your solid relationship with your children. We should question everything that is put in front of us, so we have the pride of saying, "Yeah, I look at it, and it is true (or not true)".

Having "faith" begins a psychological journey of NOT having reason, not using reason all the time in judgment and integrity and honesty. It alters our awesome method we're born with (the capacity for reason) into being obedient and "looking the other way" when we encounter things. This is often the beginning of the mind's loss of confidence and pure joy. How can we have joy if we just obey and didn't make our own minds up?

I didn't start being non-religious until I started reading the Bible myself as a young adult and, frankly, was flabbergasted by how poorly it thought of humans, and how primitive its understanding was of the universe (stars are a little ways above us in a "shell") and what we should do to unbelievers (Jesus said slay them, Luke 19:27) and how depressing the alleged ending ("apocalypse") was and how we couldn't run our own lives without outside intervention, and much more. Basically, humans were just pitiful, and I just wasn't falling for that!

We aren't pitiful. We can be honest Oak Trees in charge of our lives, needing only to keep our eyes on the facts of life – and NOT needing outside intervention.

All religions began as primitive understandings of the universe, of cause and effect, of the human mind, of morality, of the nature of humans. It was early humans' cautious attempt to make sense of a very strange world indeed. I think we can probably say that their primitiveness was understandable at the time.

But we should all know better by now.

We know from the red-shift of light that our universe is 13.7 billion years old (and wasn't created in six short days). We know from radioactive half-life decay of minerals that our own Earth is one-third that age at 4.6 billion years old – and so is the rest of our solar system, which derived from an exploding "heavy element" supernova about 5 billion years ago.

We now have millions of animal-remains specimens that solidly show that early life forms on Earth began more than 3 billion years ago, after the Earth cooled, and we know of several natural extinctions of 70% to 90% of all animals, including the Permian and Cretaceous (dinosaur) extinctions in the last 250 million years.

We know that all life has DNA – something that Jesus and Moses and Muhammad did not talk about or KNOW. We know that our own DNA is almost identical to that of chimps, making them our closest ancestral species, and that if you go back 140 million years, the shrew is the ancestor to all mammals on Earth.

After the Age of Enlightenment and the Industrial Revolution and the "Rights Revolution" and the moon landing and the wondrous devices of capitalism's inventors and the scientific understanding of what us humans are capable of, we know that the human mind is NOT pitiful It's actually a wonder – contrary to what religions and their preachers have been telling us for 3,000 years.

Children are new to this Earth, so they see things with fresh eyes, unencumbered by the traditions of superstition. They see the magnificent things above and they watch spectacular videos on them. They are no longer as likely to listen to preaching that doesn't align with what the children know to be true.

And the kids will eventually lose respect for any child or adult who makes religious claims and attempts to force their non-factual worldview on the kids. The children may not tell their religious parents that they don't like going to church or that they've lost some respect for the parents for doing so – but the disrespect is there, and the Oak Tree has lost a limb.

You Better Watch Out ... You Better Not Lie

And since we're on the subject of lying to our kids about the real nature of the world and ghosts, let's not forget the Big Three of American culture: Santa Claus, The Tooth Fairy and The Easter Bunny. (Every culture has its own mythologies.)

They are perceived by many or most American parents as harmless "white lies" for their kids. But, in fact, they are all deceptions – perhaps even pranks – that children buy into and then learn aren't true (how I wish this was the same sequence with religion!).

Lying to our children about anything, including the Big Three, sets a tone of mistrust in what we say and do. Once they figure out that we are fooling them on these three, they often wonder what ELSE we're trying to fool them about – not a good way to begin our friendship journey with our kids!

Almost every adult I've talked to has said that when they were a kid they were pretty darn upset to find out eventually that Santa didn't exist, and some kids had to experience the shame of being the only one among their friends who didn't know – and was laughed at because they didn't know.

We all love to have fun with our children and even do some agreed-upon make-believe with them, but to foist Medieval superstition myths on them without their knowledge takes a bite out of our credibility as the Honest Oak Tree.

On top of the deception of these three, some parents go even a step further, and turn the Big Three into "watchers" of their children – somewhat like alleged gods are used for with children.

"You better watch out. You better not cry. You better not pout. I'm telling you why. Santa Claus is coming to town."

Really?!

I hardly know where to begin with that little piece of condescension and cruelty.

Free kids don't have rulers, so they don't have to "watch out" for ANYONE.

People cry. What's wrong with crying?

Pouting is pathetic, yes, but if our kids are pouting, we can talk with them sympathetically to perhaps help them understand a problem. We don't threaten them with no presents from a mystery man if they pout! That's just cruel.

When my daughter was young, I told her about these Big Three make-believe things. She couldn't understand fully why adults would make them up, but she wanted to make-believe I was the Tooth Fairy and put money under her pillow when she lost a tooth. I would sneak into her room in the middle of the night and put a dollar bill under her pillow and take the bloody tooth. We had great fun doing this, but the fun was in me actually being able to be a part of agreed make-believe with my daughter.

It's time to put an end to these silly, traditional deceptions, and to enjoy straight-up communication and mutually agreed make-believe with our kids. It's far more substantial to the relationship. It's truthful. It's REAL.

So, parents, "You better watch out. You better not lie!"

Please, Santa, just stay at the North Pole and swallow your myth with some tasty eggnog.

You Know It

Life isn't about what someone else says it is. It's not about the teachings of Buddha or Zoroaster or Jesus or Moses or Shiva or Muhammad or the Dalai Lama, unless what they said passes the truth-test of our minds – and it doesn't. It isn't being "nice" to say that people can "believe what they want to believe". If what someone believes is wrong, then that will mess up their mind and actions. To tell them it's OK to believe in nonsense is, frankly, to become an "enabler".

The universe is not an unknowable place peopled with "spirits" without bodies – such a thing could not exist without nourishment. The universe simply is what it is – a vast playground for humans to look at and explore happily and benevolently.

I hope all parents will re-evaluate "faith" and religion and "gods" and fairy tales and obedience, and welcome our wonderful pirate world just as it is – for their self-full sake, and for the sake of their relationship with their doting children.

After all, it's all about you you you and them them them!

Let's Get Rational, Rational! (Sorry, ONJ)

As I said in the previous section on religion and throughout the book, our minds are built for understanding. We can put two-plus-two together like nobody's business. Our 3-pound brains can figure anything out eventually, given enough facts.

I've tried to provide a better understanding of the respect that is due to the mind of kids – and adults. It is a respect that has been lacking throughout history – for our immensely powerful rational minds.

Though kids (and adults) may sometimes act irrationally, our minds CAN be rational and WILL be rational – if we put our mind to it!

We are wonderfully built to have emotions, too, and it is those emotions that give feeling to what's in our mind – that give feeling to our life. When we see our child accomplish something that was important to them, our hearts burst with joy, because we love them. Our mind has determined that they are a very high value to us, so when we see them do something great, our heart pumps out "love juices" (sorry, couldn't think of a better way to put that!).

When a bad driver cuts us off in traffic and almost makes us wreck, we get furious because they have blithely almost hurt our highest value (ourselves) and other very high values (our kids or others). In this situation, the heart pumps out a different kind of emotional juice. Our lives are quite tangible in these moments.

Our hearts and minds are connected – but we think only with our mind, not our heart, which "only" pumps out chemicals according to what our mind has determined is good and bad to begin with.

This doesn't mean we can't "listen to our heart", of course. We SHOULD listen to our heart. But what that means is that when an emotion happens, we acknowledge it (listen to it) and then trace back that emotion to what we were thinking – to figure out what made us have the emotion, in case we didn't know already. Our emotions can be the initial clue for our Sherlock Holmes minds.

This means that if we are acting irrational or feeling anxious in certain situations or getting happy for some unknown reason, we can start sleuthing in our mind when we feel the emotion. We can use our emotions as clues to eventually "fix" ourselves. If we are getting anxious about a family get-together, we can listen to that emotion, sit down for a while, and run through scenarios in our minds until VOILA – we've figured out exactly what it is about the reunion that is troubling us. If it turns out it was, for example, a wrong judgment we had of a person who was going to be there, then we can fix that judgment and get rid of the anxiety. Fun times!

Emotions are the effect, not the cause, in our lives. They are what we feel AFTER we've determined what's right and wrong, of what's a value and what isn't, of what's an injustice or what is fairness. And to feel very strongly about something doesn't automatically mean that we are correct – or give us the right to demand, "Well, I felt strongly about that and I don't want to talk about it anymore."

We should be able to justify our comments or actions we take in our lives to ourselves and anyone else. Those thoughts and actions should be based on the facts of life, so we can be our own Oak Tree and our children's Oak Tree.

Our minds are an awful thing to waste. Let's get rational, rational!

Working 9 to 5!

"Work" has become a "four-letter word" in our society, when in actuality, work sets us free (not in the cynical Nazi sense, of course). We should enjoy our weekends, no doubt, but we shouldn't be working FOR the weekend.

Work is our productivity, the production of our minds. For lack of a better way to put it, work is our primary relationship with reality. In other words, when we get up in the morning, it is the things around us and the things in the world that we experience and plan for that are of primary importance to us.

Reality is where we live and what we think about, more than any particular thing in our lives, including others. It is what we use or change or immerse ourselves into every day of our working lives. It is and should be what we spend our most precious commodity of time on.

In the longterm, it should be even more satisfying than our loved ones or even … sex! Ahem.

What I mean by that is that we are all creative beings, each unique, each with an individual feeling and "correspondence" between our inner world and the outer world. We each have a "connection" to the world around us. We each want to do something with it, whether it is to make things or say things or write things or move things or teach things or fix things or draw things or pick-up things or trim things or style things or grow things.

THAT is the sex of life. It's what gives us identity and tells us and the world who we are. It's the reason why people usually say to us "what do you do" when they first meet us. They want to know WHO we are. They are really saying "Who are you?"

People who have a job they love are happy people, and they are usually people we all enjoy talking to, because they find their work interesting, and it gives them great pride, as it should. Our friends who are busy with their work are usually the ones we ask favors of, too – which gives truth to the adage, "If you want something done, ask a busy person to do it." Busy people LIKE being busy with their relationship to the real world.

As I said earlier, childrearing isn't primarily a job. It's an avocation that requires not so much time if we're raising our children as free people. All of us parents should have a "reality relationship" job that is outside of our kids – to fulfill our need to be self-full and to vent that unique creativity that lurks within.

Because we have kids, the work may not be 9 to 5, but what the heck. Some of us like the wee hours of the morning anyway for creativity!

"I think the girl who is able to earn her own living and pay her own way should be as happy as anybody on earth. The sense of independence and security is very sweet."
– Susan B. Anthony

The Buck Stops Here

If we are making up our own minds on everything in our lives, we are essentially saying, "Hey, the buck stops here!" No whining. No pointing fingers elsewhere when we screw up. No giving credit to others when WE are awesome. We have to be independent and enjoy our independence of mind and action – and take credit for it.

"Here" being our brain, our thoughts, our judgment, our adherence to the facts of a situation. We have the honesty and confidence to listen to others if they are trying to honestly make a point, but in the end, it's up to us to determine what's good for us.

We've been told our whole lives that we should instead listen to authority and obey authority, whether it's a religious book or a parent or an "older person" or a spouse or a religious authority or "tradition" or a family member or an administrator or a child or political correctness or an official – frankly, ANYBODY except ourselves.

But only our own mind can determine what WE want and what is good for us and what are the facts of reality that relate to our values and needs. We should be "first-handed" in our lives, not "second-handed" – relying on our rational mind, not the opinions or disapproval of others, who are not LIVING our lives for us.

And to be independent, we first have to be self-full, productive and rational, as I've mentioned in the previous sections. We have to focus on us and our own relationship with reality. We have to be our own Oak Tree. Our children will mirror our independence as well, and admire us for it. They will be less vulnerable in world where THEY make up their own minds about things.

Honesty ... Is Such a Lonely Word

Billy Joel wasn't feeling too good about people when he wrote his song, but he hit the nail on the head. Even the most honest people tend to say, "Well, there's nothing wrong with a little white lie."

Yes there is. A lie to anybody, outside of robbers and government (but I repeat myself), is basically saying, "I don't have the courage to tell the truth right now."

For example, to tell a child that we don't have the money to buy candy when we DO have the money is, frankly, just cowardice. It means we don't have the courage to deal with a situation in which we tell the truth, "Darling, I just came here to quickly get a gallon of milk and don't have time for anything else. Maybe tomorrow."

Telling the truth feels good always. The reason it feels good is that it is putting into action exactly what is in our head, so it keeps us "clean" and it says about us, "I mean what I think and say."

All of that said, there has been a quiet revolution in the last 60 years on the definition of "honesty". The author Ayn Rand says that honesty is NOT primarily about what we say to ourselves or other people. It's not "people" oriented. She says honesty is primarily about our relationship to reality. Are we being true to what's going on around us? Are we staying focused on what's going on around us? Are we keeping in mind what's important to us, our values?

I agree with Ms. Rand about this new way of looking at honesty, especially considering that reality is our primary relationship – even before our kids and our spouses and our friends and family – because it has to do with US all the time.

Under the old definition of honesty (truth to others), we would have to tell the truth to a robber asking us our PIN to our debit card before running off. Under the old definition, we HAVE to be "honest" in that situation.

Under Rand's definition, the reality of the situation is that the robber has no right to our PIN, our property, our values. We recognize the coercive threat and give him what he deserves: a false number. In this situation, we have remained self-full and honest about our relationship to reality.

The reason this new definition is important to us is it takes the fundamental focus of our lives off of other people and puts it where it's supposed to be – on us and our values, which include our kids, our other loved ones, our property and our time. All we have to do is stay focused on what's important to us in each situation.

Here Comes the Judge

Most of us have been told our whole lives that we're not supposed to judge others.

Yes we are!

Yes we do!

Yes we should!

Yes it's good!

Jesus and virtually all "thinkers" throughout history have been wrong on this subject, and the reason they were wrong is they thought we weren't "good enough" to make good judgments, and we weren't "worthy enough" to judge.

Our minds are both "good enough" and "worthy enough" to be honest, independent, courageous, loving, productive and properly judgmental.

More than that. We HAVE to judge to survive and live well. Somebody telling us not to judge, as Joel Osteen loves to do, is setting us up for a disastrous life. In fact, Osteen's statement of "don't judge" is itself a judgment – that humans aren't capable of judging well and shouldn't judge. He doesn't see his own contradiction.

With our Oak Tree self-fullness clearly in mind, we have to look at the facts of how people act around us to see if they are good for us or bad for us – and our kids. We simply can't live a good life if we don't properly judge other people. It doesn't mean we are being harsh or "selfish". It means we are trying to SURVIVE and prosper!

We have to be judge and jury for what goes on around us all the time. We have to judge ourselves, and then judge others.

If we couldn't judge, how would we judge someone to be our soulmate for life?

If we couldn't judge, what use would being the Happy Oak Tree be – because we couldn't judge our children's good Paths and bad Paths? In fact, there would be no such THING as good and bad, if we couldn't judge. Our brains would have to be blank all the time and never make any assessments at all. Boring!

If we couldn't judge, how could we have American Idol?! Kidding. Well, no, NOT kidding. We couldn't have singing judges either.

If we couldn't judge, how could we tell Uncle Bernie to stay away from our kids because he acts strange all the time?

If we couldn't judge, how would we choose a president? We wouldn't be allowed to judge candidates' good and bad qualities.

If we couldn't judge, we couldn't call a lazy co-worker lazy. They ARE!

If we couldn't judge, we'd have to be friends with drunks, thieves, liars, abusers, bullies, druggies and gamblers – because we wouldn't be "allowed" to judge them to be any of those dreadful things.

And we don't have to be perfect ourselves to judge others. That's another flaw in the PC and religious crowd that demands we don't judge. "Well, you're not perfect and never will be, so how can you judge others?"

Glad they asked. The answer is, "To survive and live well!"

OK, so we may not be perfect. That leaves room for others to judge us. That's good. Hopefully, they will tell us what they think we're doing wrong. If we agree with their "judgment", then we can happily change the way we're doing something, so we can be a Happier Oak Tree. Judgment is good for all of us and helps us correct things and live more robust lives.

And that "change" wouldn't happen if that person didn't thankfully JUDGE us. It is a natural part of life, even if it means we have to tell someone to stay away from us forever. That's harsh, but sometimes people do very bad things around us, and we have to judge them harshly, and stand by our judgment. We can't be happy when they are around – so they have to go. We have to be self-full.

But on top of all of the above, if we can't judge bad things, then we can't judge GOOD things and good people. Assessing someone to be good takes judgment of what they said and what they do.

If we can't judge, then friendship and love mean absolutely nothing – because we didn't use our judgment to pick those wonderful people and basically say, "You are awesome!"

No, judging is a very very good thing. It makes our lives safer and more fun.

After all, it's all about us us us!

Here comes the judge!

The Right Hand and The Left Hand

"Integrity" is one of those words that people have a hard time defining, and it is usually used to describe somebody with the general understanding of the Supreme Court's definition of pornography: "You know it when you see it."

Integrity is the "integration" of body and mind in action, and the integration of concepts and principles in our mind. That's a mouthful. Here's a more down-to-earth explanation.

You do what you say you'll do, and you stick with facts when dealing with the world, and you put those facts in your head in logical order, so you can use them well.

When I was doing some business a while back, I was scheduled to meet a man with whom I had a verbal agreement about the details of a business deal we were working on. That's why I agreed to meet him.

When we met, he started disagreeing with all of the details. My mouth hung open, I'm pretty sure. He sat straight-faced looking at me. I said to him, "But you said you agreed with all of this stuff." He said, "It doesn't matter what I said." I grabbed my folder and walked out without a word, while he was saying something behind me.

THAT is "disintegration" – a mind so completely dishonest that what it thinks and what it does is no longer connected, and it simply doesn't matter to him. His left hand either doesn't know what his right hand says or thinks, or it simply doesn't care. Either way, frankly, it has a frightful hint of insanity about it.

Most people are not nearly that bad, thankfully. But if we are not sticking to the facts of reality and organizing our thoughts, it can lead to trouble in action. Sometimes it's good to back off of a particularly difficult subject and "gather our wits".

And it's even worse if we are not acting on what we are rightly thinking and saying or we are acting the opposite of what we are thinking or saying. This is a nightmare for anybody, including parents – and the children who are watching them.

Our kids should be able to look at us always and think to themselves, "My mom and dad never lie and always do what they say they'll do. They've got integrity."

And we should have the pride of our own integrity as Happy Oak Trees.

Pride Isn't Just for Lions

OK, so we've heard most of the "pride" warnings in our life:

1) Pride goeth before the fall
2) With pride, there are many curses
3) It was pride that changed angels into devils

4) Is Pride the never-failing vice of fools?
5) Pride and conceit were the original sins of man

That's my shortest list in the book, thankfully so!

What many people mean by "pride" is "conceited". That is obviously horrible and self-deluded. It indicates low self-esteem propped up by braggadocio.

But we should have proper pride in our good thinking and our good acting and, well, our awesomeness. It's absolutely necessary to have pride in ourselves. If we are being awesome, why shouldn't we give ourselves a hearty pat on the back? The world can be a tough place at times, so our small and big victories that we work for should give us a lot of satisfaction – and tell us that we are doing the right things with our life to get things done well and right.

If we are being rational and productive and independent and honest and just and integrated, we should feel a great amount of pride in ourselves. It should be a personal feeling of contentment, obviously, and not something we bullhorn to the world.

It's the feeling when you get up in the morning and think, "Dang, things are going well with me and the kids and everyone else. I've got things purring after a lot of hard work. Good on ME!"

Who says pride Is just for lions?!

The Role of a Lifetime

Before I finish this book with a few last comments in the next section on getting your satisfaction, I wanted to talk about us parents being role models in all aspects of our lives. I haven't really talked about that much before because I've wanted to stress the importance of children's awesome brains and their rights to run those brains – and the fact that free kids will act independently and use their free will to make their own decisions, no matter what decisions the parents make.

But parents' being role models gives kids a tangible person they love as someone who visibly lives what they say in the realm of work, independence, honesty, justice, integrity, integration, pride and self-esteem.

On top of those valuable traits, a parent should also live their life fully and with loads of fun. To do so means also valuing physical fitness and nutrition, to show that the parent truly cares about their body and its ability to perform well in the world and not getting in the way of happiness. Our bodies are exact replicas of our minds. Messy minds means messy bodies. Clean, powerful minds means powerful bodies!

I don't think we can tell kids that we really care about having fun and being awesome if we allow our bodies to waste away or get fat – making us more prone to disease and hampering our movement in activities, and making us feel bad much of the time.

Fitness, along with the other important traits, helps make us role models for life!

I Can Get My Satisfaction

As self-full and Happy Oak Trees, we get to experience the wonderful emotions of being the "the boss of me" and being bosom buddies with our children.

We get to experience the grand satisfaction of being in charge of our lives, knowing that we are living our pirate life and honoring the rights of our children to live their pirate lives – and using only our explanations and Leverage to alter bad Paths of Least Resistance in our children.

Because we honor our children's rights, we know that whatever they choose to do with their lives, THEY chose it and get to experience their own satisfaction and awesome emotions. And we get to experience the pride of knowing that we were the ones who honored them fully in their great adventure through childhood.

If you are having some trouble with this last chapter and all the new ideas that were introduced on honesty, integrity, productivity, pride, judgment and more, I highly recommend the works of the author Ayn Rand. She is remarkably clear and rational about all of the above. She will provide a lot more insight than I have done here to help you become fully self-full.

After reading this book, you may have many questions about Oak Trees or Leverage or Paths of Least Resistance or Self-Fullness or any number of ideas I've explained, or you may just have comments and questions about how to apply all of the above to your wonderful life with your children.

If so, I hope you'll join my Facebook page "Children Have Rights" (Anny Morele) and join our lively discussions there. You will also find our Children's Rights web page link at the Facebook site or go directly to www.annymorele.com, and you are welcome to go there and join our website discussions, too.

Be strong. Be self-full. Be a Happy Oak Tree. Be YOU!

I wish you all a magnificent life – in your personal endeavors and with your lovely children!

Comments about "Children Have Rights" on Amazon

"Wow, just wow! I have been working with kids for 23 years now and have always been impressed with their capabilities. They are amazing. In all those years I have never encountered someone who holds children in the same esteem as I have – until Anny Morele, and she goes even further. Anny is the first person I have read (or even heard of) who identifies and proves that children have rights – just like us adults. Revolutionary! She takes the reader on a quick-paced adventure through the process of how this identification was made and how to implement the honoring of a child's right in a household. She convincingly proves how this will liberate both parents and children and result in a respectable, happy and fun household."
– Kino H.

"After reading this book, not only do I completely agree with the author, I feel that I have the tools and knowledge to implement this with a child. It's really quite easy! Who would've thought … raising a child doesn't have to be "hard" or "work" or a "job". Anny's approach and explanations are so on point. It's exciting knowing that once I do decide it's time for a baby I'm going to be growing my future BFF! How cool is that? It's also pretty empowering to know that I now have the tools to not "mess" my kid up – which honestly was a huge fear of mine."
– Rachel P.

*****

Anny Morele is a longtime business owner, a longtime writer, and a loving Care-Friend to her cherished daughter Kathryn.

CPSIA information can be obtained
at www.ICGtesting.com
Printed in the USA
LVOW13s1455080118
562240LV00043B/2052/P